The Daily Coyote

Coyote

A Story of Love, Survival, and Trust in the Wilds of Wyoming

Shreve Stockton

Simon & Schuster Paperbacks
New York   London   Toronto   Sydney

Simon & Schuster Paperbacks
A Division of Simon & Schuster
1230 Avenue of the Americas
New York, NY 10020

First Simon & Schuster trade paperback edition November 2009

SIMON & SCHUSTER PAPERBACKS and colophon are registered trademarks
of Simon & Schuster, Inc.

For information about special discounts for bulk purchases,
please contact Simon & Schuster Special Sales at
1-866-506-1949 or business@simonandschuster.com.

The Simon & Schuster Speakers Bureau can bring authors to
your live event. For more information or to book an event,
contact the Simon & Schuster Speakers Bureau at
1-866-248-3049 or visit our website at www.simonspeakers.com.

Designed by Nancy Singer

Manufactured in the United States of America

10   9   8   7   6   5   4   3   2   1

The Library of Congress has cataloged the hardcover edition as follows:

Stockton, Shreve.
        The daily coyote / Shreve Stockton.
        p. cm.
        1. Coydogs–Wyoming–Anecdotes. 2. Stockton, Shreve.
        I. Title.
SF429.C78 S76 2009
636.977'25–dc22   2008038728

ISBN 978-1-4165-9218-1
ISBN 978-1-4165-9220-4 (pbk)
ISBN 978-1-4165-9509-0 (ebook)

dedicated to Linda Allen,
who taught me to believe in possibility

The Daily Coyote

One

The jewels in this life are the events we do not plan; at least that is how it has always been for me. The plan was to move back to New York City—my city of screeching subways and underground jazz clubs; city of grit and noise and flower vendors on every third corner, of low-lit restaurants and Brooklyn graffiti, dirty martinis and expensive jeans; where music exits every doorway and window and car. New York, where the city lights under cover of clouds give the night sky an orange glow; where eight million people swarm just inches from one another.

I had left New York, the city of my passions, for two years in San Francisco, a transition so stressful, it triggered severe abdominal pain and debilitating depression, which, after six excruciating months, I finally diagnosed as gluten intolerance. After healing physically and emotionally and learning how to cook, I decided to write a book about this common, misunderstood condition to fill the void of resources on the market at the time.

The week I got my book contract, the apartment building I was living in burned to the ground after someone poured gasoline through the mail slot in the front door of the building next to mine and lit it. The fire destroyed both buildings and killed two of my neighbors that night. I spent two weeks sleeping on the floor at a friend's house while looking for a place to live, then moved to an obscure hilltop neighborhood and, because my new home sat far from public transportation, bought a Vespa scooter with the money I was saving on rent. I wrote my book in a tiny garden apartment overlooking the city, taking daily trips to the grocery store and farmers' market on my Vespa, inventing the recipes that would fill my book. When *Eating Gluten Free* hit the shelves, I knew my time in San Francisco was nearing an end. The time had come to return East.

A wild hare grew into a wild adventure as I pondered how to get my Vespa to New York City. Acting on a daydream, I decided to ride my Vespa across the country and have my belongings shipped once I got settled in New York. Despite nearly everyone in my life urging me otherwise, I set out alone, on the first day of August 2005, to cross the United States on my 150cc Vespa ET4—a trip that lasted two months to the day and covered six thousand miles.

On my ride across America, I took a sweeping path through Wyoming and fell in love at first sight, love at the very border. I felt magnetized to the land, to the red dirt and the Bighorn Mountains and the wide-openness I had no idea still existed in this country. The landscape around the Bighorns is like an ocean on pause, rolling with the subtle colors of rust and sage and gold, stretching to every horizon. These mountains are unlike other mountain ranges. While the Tetons are fangs of stone and Rainier is an ice cream sundae, the Bighorns are sloped and subtle, built of some of the oldest exposed rock in the world; rock that has existed, in its current form, for over three billion years. There is exquisite power in their permanence.

I crossed the Bighorns in awe, in reverie, and camped at their base for a night. As I rode east the next day, toward South Dakota, a violent debate raged inside me. I longed to stay in Wyoming, and was tormented at the thought of leaving it behind. I considered ending the trip then and there, going so far as to stop at the Sheridan library to read the local classifieds. But I continued on. I assumed I would click back into New York City, my city, the moment I arrived.

I didn't, and I knew within days that I wouldn't. The country had put its spell on me. One lazy, late fall morning, a week into my confused and disillusioned reunion with New York, I took a friend's laptop to a nearby coffee shop, needing to dream. I searched the internet for Wyoming rentals. The Bighorns held my heart, and I typed in the names of the tiny towns that lay scattered around them. I found one house listed, a furnished four-bedroom on seventeen acres in Ten Sleep, a town that lay just south of my route across Wyoming. Though I'd not been through that particular town, I contacted the owner and met with her daughter, who happened to be living in New York, and a week later, I mailed a deposit for the rental, sight unseen. I bought a one-way ticket to California, bought a Ford with more primer than paint from two gangsters in San Jose, filled it with all of my belongings that fit and gave the rest away, and in the blustery, pale days of early November, started driving toward my new, unknown home.

If someone had told me, even three months prior, that I would move, willingly, to a town of three hundred people, I would have told them they needed some Windex for their crystal ball. It was a drastic move, one not based in logic, security, experience, or anything other than unignorable desire, dictated solely by my passion for Wyoming's land. I fall in love with places the way I fall in love with men. Actually, that's not the precise truth. I fall deeper, more ardently in love with places than I have with any man, and will give myself over to a place in a way I have never given myself to a person.

I've never felt roots, have never felt conventionally attached to family or religion or any societal group. In one of his novels, Salman Rushdie wrote a great passage about "those born not belonging," and I've had it framed on my desk for years—not only is it exquisitely written, it is the only thing I've ever totally identified with. I've identified with a piece of paper more than any person or place? I raise an eyebrow just writing that, it's so stark and sad and a little romantic, but more than all that, it's true. I have spent my life running by myself, for myself, and this is the way I got myself to Wyoming.

My family and friends responded to my move in every way possible, from a shaking of the head and writing it off as frivolous irresponsibility to support and a keen jealousy. Yet most of the people who knew me well chalked it up to *what else would we expect from Shreve.* In high school, I was voted Most Likely to Wake Up in a Strange Place, and not entirely because I was a straight-A delinquent often under some influence. I have always roamed; always seized every opportunity to take off and explore, whether it was wandering the woods in the dark as a child, traveling down the coast of California on the Green Tortoise bus when I was fifteen, or jumping in my car and driving, somewhere, anywhere, until I had to be back to school or work on Monday morning. My travels were never attempts to escape; the goal was to explore, to go, because I could. Great unknowns were out there to be seen, felt, experienced; this was what life meant to me, this was what life was for. And nothing meant more to me than my freedom.

I moved to a speck of a town in an area where I had only spent one day because I knew it was the only way I would be happy. Logistics did not enter into the equation—I didn't know how I'd make a living, but I knew I would, somehow, because I had to. I arrived in Ten Sleep with a small amount of savings; royalty checks from the cookbook had a habit of showing up in the mail at the precise moments when I desperately needed them. Though my overhead was much lower than it had been in the city and though I had a few freelance graphic design clients I continued to work for from a distance, generating steady income was an issue I needed to address rather immediately.

To be honest, I was filled with trepidation when I got within fifty miles of Ten Sleep. I had no idea what I was driving into. I knew no one, knew nothing of the town or even the landscape of that particular area. I hoped to love it, hoped it would turn out to be as right as it felt, and it was. The house was much too big for me but the rent fit and the location was ideal, two miles out of town, in a rural wonderland where not even telephone poles were visible in two directions. The seventeen acres of pasture and red dirt draws bordered the BLM, untouched public land regulated by the Bureau of Land Management, accessible only on foot or by horseback. I had a handful of nearby neighbors, all of whom were shockingly kind and understandably curious. They wondered what I was doing here, and just how long I would last.

In moving to Ten Sleep, I felt like I had moved to another planet. It was more common to see cows on the road than vehicles; it was a sixty-mile drive just to buy a piece of fruit; the only radio station played Top 40 country; and most of the men wore cowboy hats and had more guns than a city girl has shoes. "Ten Sleep" is the English translation of the original Native American name; this spot had been halfway between two large Indian camps, and from here, it was a ten-day's journey to either of them—each camp was "ten sleeps" away. The town was

three blocks long, but Ten Sleep extended for many, many miles to the North and South. This was ranching country, sheep and cattle. Ranches dotted the county highways; the land between them wide, devoted to livestock.

It's hard to stay hidden in a town of three hundred people. Ten Sleep was filled with a little bit of everything as far as demographics go, and age did not seem important to anyone as far as defining friendships. There were retired couples, young families, middle-aged singles, and a smattering of people my age. I met people easily, at the library, the post office, the coffeeshop, the gas station, and the saloon. Which pretty much covered all the establishments in town, not counting the eight churches. The Methodist church, a burgundy steel building that sat at the edge of a sheep pasture, was on the route between my house and town and boasted a readerboard which inspired many of my daily meditations. *"Soul Food . . . More Lasting Than Fast Food,"* it read when I first drove into Ten Sleep.

It was winter when I moved to Ten Sleep, and often it was so cold my truck wouldn't start so I'd walk the two miles to the library or the post office. I followed the tarred cracks up the center line; for the most part, the road was my own. I got to know several of my neighbors thanks to these walks to town, for when they passed me on the road they would stop, even though we had never met, and offer me a ride. I was grateful for the lifts, especially when carrying boxes home from the post office, and happy for the spontaneous introductions.

In the beginning I felt alone. Not lonely and not in a bad way, but alone because I was in awe of the differences, and no one I knew had any idea what the transition was like. My friends and family from the cities and suburbs couldn't begin to comprehend my new reality, and the locals couldn't fathom what it was like to move into this life from where I had come. Yet I was too stimulated to feel nervous about integrating, and I immersed myself in the place. Everything was new; everything was so different from anything I had known. At times, I'd step outside and lean back against the wall of the house, my lids curtaining my eyes. The majesty of the land that lay in front of me was often difficult for me to bear; it was too pure, too beautiful. It took effort, presence, simply to be in it, to be part of it, to gaze out upon the landscape or out into the stars, to breathe air this uncontaminated. My lungs and my blood didn't know what to do with all the oxygen. It took a period of adjustment to grow comfortable with this kind of good, this kind of real, this kind of beauty after a life surrounded with plastic and pollution, and it made me a little high.

In the city, space is shared with thousands upon thousands and the only thing that's truly yours is time; therefore time is precious, rationed. Conversations are direct and to the point; this isn't rudeness, it's conservation of time. And because a person's living space is their only personal space—once it's left, space is shared, as the sidewalks, subways, offices, cafés, and bars are all crammed with others—visits are preceded by a phone call or an invitation. Showing up is faux pas.

In the country, the inverse is true. Space is vast and very often empty—one can drive a hundred miles and pass just six other trucks. Human contact is never a given, and so time is spent luxuriously with others. Running errands can take all day, as people stop to chat with those they meet along the way. I realized I ended phone conversations prematurely by signing off after conducting the actual business of the call without allowing for the leisurely banter that can go on for another twenty minutes. I had to quickly get used to people stopping by unannounced, had to quickly learn not to resent these unscheduled visits but learn that this was considered neighborly. And though I felt uncomfortable dropping by friends' and neighbors' houses without calling first, I made myself do it, because I knew it was welcomed.

Even on the road, the human connection is honored. Cars are not barriers or personal bubbles as they are in the city. Drivers make eye contact when they pass one another and nearly everyone waves, stranger or not. Even in separate vehicles, there is an intimacy; it is an acknowledgment of another human in this vast scape, and of treating them as a comrade.

The paradox is that while time with others was a thing to be savored and spent as slowly and sweetly as honey pouring, words themselves were not wasted, at least not by the men. Early on, when talking with a cowboy, I found myself trying to calculate the longest possible way to say whatever I had to say, because with my nature and his, the spoken words were rare. How can "yes" turn into a sentence of twelve syllables or more? Not only are words spare, phrasing is sparse like the landscape. *"To be"* does not exist in the spoken language. "The cows need fed," one would say, or "Which fence needs fixed?" In conversation, nothing said is a definite, even if it was definite. "He's prob'ly not comin' up this weekend" meant he's not coming up. "Maybe this afternoon" was an affirmative, as in, plan for this afternoon. Such were the subtle, interpersonal differences that took time just to recognize and name. I must have seemed brash and fast and strange, but slowly the rhythm of the way of things here naturally took its hold on my being.

There were other, more obvious differences between my new Wyoming reality and that which I had left behind. There was no curbside garbage pickup (nor were there curbs), and hauling my trash to the dump was a thrill, and the view from the dump was one of the most breathtaking I'd ever seen. Open land rolled out to the horizon, the Bighorns arching in deep blue curves to meet the skyline. Antelope roamed the outskirts of the trash piles while hawks scavenged. It was shocking to see a section labeled "Dead Animals," which I was compelled to investigate. Skinned carcasses of animals I couldn't determine lay in a deep dirt hole; a few dead sheep, larger than I would have expected, were crumpled near the edge. On one trip, I had my initiation to mud. The red dirt has a high clay content and the mud is slick and bottomless, more treacherous, in my opinion, than ice, and when trying to accelerate out of a slide, I got my truck stuck. I delicately jumped out, sinking to my ankles as I tried to tiptoe to each front tire to lock the hubs for four-wheel drive. Four-wheel drive got me out of the mud, but from then on, I planned my dump trips when I knew the ground was frozen or when it had been hot and dry enough to harden.

Recycling was as novel in Ten Sleep as dump trips were to me. My friend Gloria had invited me for a holiday dinner with her family and her sister's family. I was helping in the kitchen, and after fixing the dessert I had been assigned, I started rinsing the tin cans in the sink. I slowly turned around, feeling the unnerving sensation of multiple eyes staring at me. Gloria's sister, the most outspoken of the bunch, said, "Um, Shreve? Why are you washing the garbage?"

Specific addresses were never used; instead, landmarks were given for directions. I have been told, "Take your first right after you cross the cattle guard," and, "Turn left at the haystack," and after two prayer-filled return trips, I realized how important it was, when setting out to visit a friend, to make sure I had more than an eighth of a tank of gas.

Every ten days or so, I drove across the stark badlands to the grocery store, and though I still took issue with having to make a two-hour commitment to get groceries, I devoured the desolate, intricate landscape with my eyes and pondered the lyrics of country-western songs on the radio. *"If heaven were a pie, it would be cherry . . ."* What does this *mean*?

I was invited to my first branding. A dozen people, two more on horseback, and fifty calves at a time filled a long, dusty pen. The men

on horseback took turns roping calves by the neck or leg. Then someone on the ground rushed in to drop the calf on its side, holding it
down by the head and undoing the rope while another person grabbed
the calf's top hind leg and sat in the dirt with one foot pushed against
the bottom hind leg under the tail. Once the calf was securely down,
more people swooped in, moving quickly and efficiently without getting in each other's way. Some gave shots and others branded the calf
with irons heated in a fire built in a 55-gallon drum. Smoke plumed
from the burning hair; the calf screamed, its eyes bugging out and its
pointy lavender tongue lolling in the dirt.

I was a wallflower, taking it all in. There was so much activity, so
many noises and smells and people and calves. The horses were stoic
workers, quick on their feet, responsive, essential members of the team.
It was an exquisite choreography. I didn't want to interfere; I was completely ignorant as to what to do. About an hour into it, Carol, the
rancher's wife and the one who had invited me, came over to talk and
to lure me into the action. After chatting for a while, Carol said, "If
you want a guy to wrestle with, he's the one," and she nodded toward a
strong, blond cowboy my age. *If I want someone to wrestle with?* I repeated
in my head. I couldn't help but give her a quizzical stare. In the next
moment, we burst out laughing together, as I realized she meant "wrestle calves" and she realized I thought she meant it as a euphemism, as
in "get it on."

I did end up wrestling a few calves with the cowboy. When small
calves were roped, I was ushered in. He took the head and I took the
hind end, though I think he probably could have held these small calves
on his own. It took all my strength to keep hold of the calf's ankle as
it squirmed wildly as it was branded. Sometimes the hair caught briefly
on fire, and there was an immediate cloud of thick smoke and the smell
of singed hair was all that existed for a moment. The odor subsided but

hung in the air, refreshed as each calf was branded. The calves recovered remarkably quickly from their brief trauma, called out a *moo* to their mothers, and frolicked and played outside the fence once they were released. If only humans could get over their pain so immediately.

In early December, at the library holiday party and silent auction, Karen, the librarian, generously took it upon herself to introduce me to everyone that I had not already met. She introduced me to the principal of the town school, who, after hearing my background, offered me a job right then and there as a substitute teacher, for which they had a desperate need. I was terrified to accept. I'd never taught before, but I needed a job. And so I took the state exam for my substitute credential, got fingerprinted, and began working at the school in January. My first subbing assignment was for the fifth- and sixth-grade combined class, and I was so nervous I asked the teacher if I could come in the day before to observe. I had no idea what to expect, or what would be expected of me.

I was immediately subbing an average of three days a week, which gave me enough money to live on and enough time to work on my writing. Kindergarten through twelfth grade was all in one building; seventy-eight students total. Kids rode the bus as far as thirty-five miles each way to reach the school from their families' ranches, and there was a familial relationship between the children—sweet, tolerant, helpful, and worshipful, depending on their age. Some classes had as many as twenty children, some as few as four. I subbed for everything—from first grade to shop class, math, gym, and high school history, and most often for the fifth- and sixth-grade combined class. I formed tight relationships with the kids, relationships that were trusting, humorous, honest. I became incredibly invested in the students, and they knew it.

After a month of subbing, I sat in my pasture and actually gave thanks for being broke, knowing I'd never have started teaching if I had not been so desperate for money; and thus never would have discovered how much I adored it, how much I adored the kids.

As I earned respect from the kids in the school, I got street cred among the locals for lasting the winter without getting old, getting lonely, or going crazy. Apparently, most people who come in from elsewhere don't last. My days of sushi and fresh carrot juice were long gone; instead of sidewalks there was ice, snow, mud, or prickly weeds, depending on the season. I didn't care. This was Wyoming, this was where I got to live. Where I could stand in the wide open space with no one around, wear dirty jeans and only brush my hair if I felt like it, and fall a little bit in love with every man wearing a cowboy hat.

Thanks to my broken-down truck, I had come to enjoy my explorations afoot. The land was so quiet, especially in winter; snow shrouded the hills and coated the roads with a thick layer of white. Pavement disappeared; automobiles were a rare sight. My time outside became my time of peace and release, away from responsibility and away from my work, when I got out of my head and let myself free.

One evening after teaching, I went for a run to release the energy of the school day before a night of writing. I started north on the dirt road past my house, slowly letting go and letting the peace of the landscape enter. A red pickup cruised past, two cowboys grinning at me from behind the windshield. I gave them a low wave and trotted on through the dry weeds beside the road. I leapt over a culvert and caught a glimpse of a small, black mass up ahead; as I drew closer, I saw it was the small, shiny body of a newborn calf curled up next to the fence. A black mother cow, larger than her own shadow, stood guard nearby. The pair was slightly removed from the other cows dotting the pasture and I stopped and stood at the fence—I had never seen a newborn calf before. It was curled up like a dog, its large eyes closed, peaceful in the late light of day.

A honk snapped me from my reverie. Cresting a hill in the pasture was the same red pickup I had passed on the road.

"I bet this is these cowboys' calf," I immediately thought to myself. "I hope they aren't angry that I'm looking at it." Two cowboys getting mad at me for looking at their calf? The city was ingrained into my psyche, where respect is shown by giving others a wide berth and keeping out of their business. I turned on my heel and started off down the road. A loud "Hey!" from one of the cowboys stopped me in my tracks.

The truck, piled high with hay, sat idling in the pasture with the cowboys standing beside it, just on the other side of the fence from where I stood on the road.

"You wanna feed with us?" one of the men asked with a smile.

He had dark hair and eyes, and wore a light gray cowboy hat and a thick moustache.

"Sure," I said, with a nonchalant shrug of my shoulders, but couldn't help smiling back.

Moustache helped me climb over the barbwire fence, pulled out a pocket knife, and flicked it open and handed it to me. I stared at the knife and held on to it, not knowing why I had it, hoping the reason would soon make itself evident. Meanwhile, the other cowboy, decked in worn jeans, a snap shirt, and a gray wool vest, climbed up to the top of the stack of hay bales that filled the back of the pickup. Once up there, he reached his arm down to me, a signal that I was to join him on top of the hay. We locked arms. I looked up and into the bluest eyes I'd ever seen in my life, eyes that were like rips through all matter to show the bluest, brightest sky of the beyond. The color seemed impossible.

Moustache got in the truck and drove us out into the pasture. Blue Eyes looked at me and said, "He didn't give you gloves?"

"No," I said, unsure of why I needed gloves to go with the knife I still clutched in my hand.

"Here," he said, "take one of mine."

And so I put his leather glove on my left hand, tried to keep my balance on the bumpy pile of hay, and watched him to see what I was supposed to be doing.

Blue Eyes opened his pocketknife, sliced through the two strands of yellow twine that held each bale together, and deftly flaked off chunks of hay to feed the stream of black cows that were now following the truck en masse. I scratched at the hay bales in front of me, trying to find the twine to cut, then heaved off clumps as well as I could manage. Wayward bits of hay stabbed through my lycra running tights and scratched my thighs and the dry alfalfa leaves stuck to the fibers of my fleece sweatshirt, but I had no time to notice that my attire was inappropriate. We worked silently and fast, moving bale by bale. The glove was too big for me, and I found it easier to cut the strings, then stab the open knife into another bale to hold it while I used both hands to push sections off the first. After working three successful bales, I lost the knife. I frantically scanned the bales around me, shamed and embarrassed, dreading having to say anything to Blue Eyes. But I couldn't find it. Sheepishly, I turned to him.

"I can't find the knife," I said. "That's bad, isn't it?"

I thought if it went off the truck it could stab a cow in the foot or the mouth; what I didn't yet know was that a man's knife is an extension of himself. Blue Eyes just said, "Hmmm," and started helping me look for it. We turned circles on our tiny island of hay and to my great relief, Blue Eyes spotted the knife, stabbed in one of the remaining bales, camouflaged against the spiky, icy-green hay.

When we finished, Moustache and Blue Eyes congratulated me on doing a great job, which I certainly hadn't, and invited me to dinner with them. I declined for I still had writing I hoped to get done that night. They insisted on driving me back to my house, and so I squeezed in the pickup between them and laughed the entire way home.

Three days later, I was driving back from the neighboring town of Hyattville, where I had ended up after following the gorgeous scenery and the snow-covered dirt roads beyond my house. As I neared home, I saw Blue Eyes in his pasture, throwing hay off the back of his hay-laden truck, the evening ritual. But I could see through his windshield that no one was in the driver's seat. As the truck approached the far fence, Blue Eyes jumped off the back, ran to the driver's door, and hopped in. The truck turned in a loose arc, headed back the way it had come. After a few moments, Blue Eyes hopped out of the moving truck and leapt back up on the back, where he continued to work through the bales. I sat in my truck on the side of the road, perplexed, curious. When he finished, Blue Eyes got in his truck, turned in another loose curve, and pulled out onto the road next to me and parked, window to window. "What was that ballet?" I asked. He told me Moustache had been visiting and helped him feed cows during his stay, but that he had returned home to another part of the state. He said when he didn't have anyone to drive for him, he tied the steering wheel and put the truck in low gear so that it drove itself across the long pasture while he fed from the back, and that he jumped between truck bed and cab when he needed to turn before hitting a fence.

"You feed every night?" I asked.

"Yes," he said.

"I'll drive for you," I said, an offer of assistance that came completely out of the blue, especially for someone who hated routine as much as I. Yet it came out so naturally. I was getting the hang of being neighborly.

"Seriously," I said. "Call me when you want to feed in the evenings and I'll be ready."

"But I don't have your phone number," he said.

I didn't know his name and I knew he didn't know mine.

"Well," I said, "I'll give it to you."

An accidental friendship bloomed between us. We spent only twenty minutes a day with each other, but spent them every day, and a certain intimacy grew on its own. I helped Mike feed cows almost every evening for the rest of the winter and through the spring, until he took the cows up the mountain where they grazed on summer pasture. And though I had an innate aversion to structure, that tiny bit of routine in my life was something I grew to enjoy, something I looked forward to. Mike loaded his truck with hay, swung by my house and picked me up, and we slowly drove to his corrals, picking up the conversation where we had been the day before, learning about each other as much by our manner as by our words, opening up to where we were that day in ourselves, in our world, or just in that particular moment.

I loved watching him throw hay. I'd take a tight grip on the steering wheel and trust I was driving a straight line, ignoring the windshield for the rearview mirror where I could watch him in the back of the truck, the movements of his thighs in his Wranglers, his shoulders, his tapered waist, his hands in work-worn leather gloves. He always wore a button-up shirt tucked in; a wool vest over it if it was cold, sleeves rolled up if it was warm. And the way his jeans fit was enough to kill me. The sun was always low but hung above the horizon; dust kicked up by the cows created a haze that made everything seem more surreal, more real.

Our time together lengthened gradually, consistently, with the help from a glowing sunset stretching across the evening sky, or an orphan calf to bottle feed, or a warm breeze to simply enjoy after winter's claw.

"Well, I guess it's that time," he'd say, after we had leaned against the rail fence for an extra twenty minutes.

"Yeah," I'd reply. "It's that time."

And then he'd say some cowboy thing like, "The worst part of my day is when I have to take you home," with the cows and the dust around him and the sun setting and the sky all milky blue, and I'd swoon inside and smile in spite of myself all night.

Eventually, though we each fought against it, we fell in love. He had told me early on that his older daughter, Tracy, died seven years earlier, when she was twelve, in a four-wheeler accident. He said he had vowed never to open his heart again so that he would never hurt like that again. I had my own version of that commitment. Love was not a goal of mine; it complicated my freedom. Yet as Spring bloomed in the land, the subtle effects of our unexpected connection took their hold, and soon, it overtook us.

Mike was not a rancher. He ran about fifty cows, which is a very small operation in comparison to the ranches in the area. Mike's career was with Wildlife Services. He was a government trapper, employed by the United States Department of Agriculture to protect livestock by killing coyotes.

Mike killed for a living, which he readily admitted with no remorse or apology. Though an agent of death, he did not kill with abandon; he took his role as a protector of livestock seriously, killing the coyotes that were an immediate threat. He firmly believed that if his job did not exist, ranchers and those working on sheep and cattle operations would take the matter into their own hands, setting out poison and trapping without expertise, killing every animal around.

People who hunt coyotes randomly for sport or with poor technique can actually exacerbate the predation problem, as a wounded coyote is more dangerous than a healthy one. Mike had seen everything from three-legged coyotes to coyotes that had had their lower jaw shot off. Unable to catch rabbits as they would in their prime, these coyotes search out easy

prey, and the easiest prey are lambs and newborn calves. And if, in the spring and early summer, when coyote pairs are raising their pups together, the female is killed and her mate remains alive, the male will support the litter himself. Alone in the task, he turns to young stock as the most efficient prey to feed his young. Mike believed he actually saved coyotes along with livestock in the manner he did his job–killing only in sensitive areas, being smart about how he did it, and doing it incredibly well.

We had many discussions about his work. Though hundreds of lambs and calves are killed and eaten by coyotes each year, I argued that predation should be looked at as the Nature Tax–that ranchers give a certain percentage of their capital to the government in taxes, and they should expect to give up a certain percentage to Nature. But there is a war between humans and predators–for land to call their territory and for the animals off which they live: cattle, sheep, deer, and elk. Most ranchers and hunters would prefer there be less or none of the wild predators, coyotes and mountain lions and wolves. People feel entitled to take the land, the resources, and the wilderness as their own without giving up anything to the land they are running on. Predators survive off what men want to keep as their own; man does not want to share. And so man becomes the ultimate predator with a singular goal, and the element of competition makes it easy to say, "So let's kill 'em," without any question or qualm.

Mike killed coyotes through a number of means–snares; foothold traps; from the ground with a rifle; and with a shotgun out of a small, low-flying airplane. I asked him what it felt like to make eye contact with a coyote and then raise his gun and fire, watch it fall, see it die. He broke our eye contact to look out the window, said he didn't feel, didn't think about it; he blocked that part out, just did what he had to do, acted only, felt nothing.

. . .

My second week in Ten Sleep, I had been driving around exploring and passed a tiny, rustic log cabin with a blue tin roof and fell in love with it from the road. "One day," I thought, "I'll live in a cabin like that." I gazed at the little cabin every time I drove by it, filled with a delicious longing, full of dreams to live there. Once I started feeding cows with Mike, I learned that he had built that cabin. It sat at the base of his property, and he told me he built it as "a practice run" before building his log home, and he meant it to be a tack shed. When the lease was about to come up on the house I was renting, Mike asked me to move in with him. We were standing in my yard and I started laughing. "No way," I said, "but I'll move into the cabin!"

The cabin sat at the western edge of his forty-acre property, on a small hill just off the road. The driveway went past the cabin, up and around two large hills, hugging the contours of the land. Mike's house was at the top, and overlooked hundreds of gorgeous, unobstructed acres of BLM to the east, all the way to the mountains. It was less than a ten-minute walk between his house and the cabin, but they did not share a line of sight; the arrangement of the buildings and the landscape provided both proximity and privacy.

Mike spent a month trying to talk me out of my cabin fantasy—he truly believed the cabin was unfit to live in and didn't see how I would possibly be happy there. I countered every argument, practically begging, reminding him that the cabin had been calling to my soul for a year. When he saw I was determined, he offered to show me the inside of the cabin as I had never been inside, convinced that seeing the space in all its lonely disrepair would change my delusional mind.

It was a 12 × 12-foot log cabin with a rough, open loft over half it and a hand-hewn wood ladder leading up to the loft. On the main floor, there were two small windows on the north and south walls, a rusty woodstove in one corner, and an L-shaped counter in the opposite corner. The walls were half chinked, as if someone had started the job and then forgot about it, never to return. Chinking, the strip of material between the logs, is applied to seal any air gaps. In modern log homes, it is a material similar to caulking; in this case, it was cement. The ceiling was the roof itself—corrugated tin nailed straight to the support beams that angled down from the ridgepole. There were mouse droppings everywhere, and dusty red dirt coated every log and beam. Mike's plan failed; I saw the beauty through the desolate mess.

I learned how to mix concrete in a five-gallon bucket and, using two small trowels, finished chinking the inside of the cabin; a steep learning curve there, but rather simple once I got the hang of it. I had sheets of two-inch Styrofoam insulation delivered from the lumberyard and cut them into panels which I nailed to the batten beams to insulate the roof. I borrowed Mike's shop vac and sucked up all the dirt and mouse residue and then washed every log and beam by hand. I made curtains for the windows and made curtain rods by whittling the bark off long branches. I bought three thick, full-length wool coats at a secondhand store for six dollars each, then cut them up into rectangles of fabric which I sewed together to make a gorgeous wool rug for the floor. I set up my bed in the corner diagonal from the woodstove and my desk and computer opposite that, and had my kitchen area in the space defined by the built-in counter. I used the loft as a lounge area, full of pillows to lie against, and organized my paperwork, books, and clothes on long, low shelves that Mike made for me out of scrap lumber.

There was electricity and a phone line running to the cabin, and I had high-speed internet hooked up through the phone company. I had plumbing in a lean-to outside during the warm months, and the woodstove was my only form of heat during the cold ones. I moved into the cabin in October and dropped five pounds in two weeks, calories burned from shivering until I mastered the art of building and maintaining a fire; I had never built a fire before. I cooked on a hotplate in the summer and on the woodstove in the winter, and when my plumbing was turned off to prevent the pipes from freezing, I had a very rudimentary outhouse situation and got water from the hose that fed the horse trough. Pretty much everyone thought I was insane when I moved into the cabin, but I adored it.

Mike refused to take money for rent because, as he put it, he couldn't honestly take my money in exchange for what he considered an uninhabitable hovel. So I took it upon myself to work as his hired hand in lieu of rent, feeding cows in the winter and irrigating in the summer and doing whatever needed done in the meantime, and I snuck his truck away whenever I could and filled it with gas.

Mike and I spent another winter feeding cows together, but this year was different from the first. Early in the season, I asked Mike on a whim if he would drive so that I could throw the hay. I hadn't done it since our first meeting, but I had watched him for so long I knew the procedure. I tied my hair back with baling twine, tucked in my shirt and climbed up on the hay. I was hooked within minutes. I loved being on the back of the truck, in the air, steadily moving the bales to feed. Cutting the twine, rhythmically sheafing off hay a quarter-bale at a time, spacing it evenly across the pasture. It became my meditation; when I was feeding, I was focused, free. I asked Mike if he'd be interested in trading jobs, which he didn't argue, happy to relax in the driver's seat with the radio and the heater while I tossed hay. When the occasional blizzard hit, Mike forced me to drive and took my place in the wind and the snow, either out of chivalry or masculine bravado, I was never sure which; and on calm, balmy days, he rolled down the windows and cranked the radio so I had music to work by. After I had been feeding for about two straight weeks, he gave me a pocketknife of my own. Moving the seventy-pound bales in the back of the truck gave my scrawny arms the beginnings of muscle, and I started accompanying Mike to the haystack to help load the truck as well. At first I could only move the bales laterally, but my strength increased with the daily work and I got to where I could stack the bales three high, head level. When I crossed that muscle threshold, I did a little dance.

Spring arrived slowly and humbly; first the Spring winds, then Spring itself. The winds viciously tore across my cabin and through every unsealed crevice; the tin roof rattled and shook. The sound of the rattling tin was horrendous, like lying on the pavement and having an eighteen-wheeler speed by. During one morning of rain and sustained forty-mile-per-hour winds, a panel of tin blew off my roof. It remained attached only at the peak. I didn't want to call Mike, didn't want him to have to climb up on the roof in the wind and rain, so I did it myself. I used a log as a step stool and swung myself onto the roof of the lean-to next to the cabin, and from there, climbed up the cabin roof with a pocketful of nails and hammered the tin back down.

Easter came in early April, the one holiday I get excited about; it represents new life and new beginnings, rebirth, resurrection: what is always possible inside us. It is a reminder of the power we have to transform ourselves and our lives, the growth that is always possible, lying latent in each of us all the time. And then, of course, there are the baby animals. Late Easter afternoon, Mike and I drove down to the haystack to load hay as we did every afternoon. Mike picked up a bale off the ground and five tiny baby bunnies ran out from under it. I was overcome with excitement, and stood there pointing and gushing, "Look! Bunnies! Babies! Oh my God! Baby bunnies!"

Mike, being more even-keeled, scooped up one of the baby cotton-tails and handed it to me, and I stood there in the hay cradling the tiny baby bunny. Its little body fit in one hand with room to spare and its front feet and tiny fluff of tail were each the size of my pinky fingernail. It had long, thin ears folded back against its body, a snow white belly, grayish tan fur, and a perfect diamond-shaped patch of white on the crown of its head between its ears. It was a surprisingly mellow little bunny; it curled up in my hand and let me pet it and wiggled its nose. Mike put the hay bale back where it had been so the bunnies could keep their home, and though secretly I wanted to keep it, I let the bunny go and it hopped into a crevice of hay. We had moved over sixty tons of hay from this haystack, and Easter was the one day we saw bunnies.

Spring is a busy season for Mike. Calves and lambs are born and are most vulnerable to predators, and the coyotes have litters of their own young to feed. One mild afternoon near the end of April, Mike pulled up in front of my cabin. When I went outside to greet him, he slid open the dog box in the bed of his pickup, and on tiptoes, I peered over the edge of the truck to look. Crouched inside the box, clumsily swaddled in a denim shirt, was a baby coyote.

I said nothing but turned to Mike, staring a question into his eyes. He said he had shot a pair of coyotes that had been killing a rancher's sheep. He walked around looking for the den—because this time of year, when the pups have been born and are dependent on their parents, he follows tracks in the dirt until he finds the den, then sticks a gas cartridge in the hole to kill the pups instantly so they do not die slowly of starvation. He said he found the den, and when he crouched down to smoke it, he saw this pup, its eyes barely opened, sitting at the edge of the hole. He said that something too strong to ignore compelled him to scoop up the tiny pup and put it in his pocket; then he went about his work gassing the rest of the pups in the den, and drove here to see me.

He said he didn't understand what came over him; that he hadn't done this in the eighteen years he'd had this job, but here, here was a coyote pup and it was for me. Before he drove up the hill to his house, he said, "If you don't want to take care of it, or it gets to be a problem, let me know and I'll drown it in the water tank."

Two

The coyote pup lay curled up in the back of Mike's truck, its eyes closed, its head between its front paws. Mike reached into the dog box as if he were collecting eggs from his chickens and brought the male pup out into the light, holding it between us. The pup remained nestled in a ball, tiny and vulnerable in Mike's hand. I stroked it with my fingertip. I was overcome with a mixture of absolute wonder and a small but very honest resentment. The baby coyote was darling; defenseless and helpless. The baby coyote was a responsibility, a commitment. The baby coyote was covered with fat, brown fleas.

"I can't believe it," was all I could say, as I gently, rhythmically, stroked the coyote. My finger moved slowly and softly over the coyote's head while in my mind, thoughts raced like streaks of fire. The responsibility for another was something I took seriously and did not have much practice in. I was flooded with the ramifications—if I did not take care of this pup, he would die; if I did, my life would dramatically change and would be governed, in large part, by the coyote, for as long as he was in my care. Mike had, with this unexpected delivery, put me in a difficult and uncomfortable position. While he could carry on with his life in the way it always had been regardless of what happened to this coyote, I was being pushed into a moral and personal debate. And though Mike knew me well enough for him to understand the precise internal conflict his spontaneous act would instigate, I doubt it was something he realized he was doing. It didn't matter. A choice confronted me in the softly breathing form of the coyote in his palm. I either had the death of this baby on my conscience or a wild coyote pup to raise, in my cabin, with my cat.

I was not looking for a pet when I got Eli; I was looking for a way to take care of the mouse problem that was slowly overtaking my rental house during my first summer in Ten Sleep. I didn't want to use poison in the house because I didn't want to affect the birds and animals that might eat the poisoned mice, and I didn't want to use traps because I didn't want to touch them. I decided a cat would be the ideal solution, and put the word out that I was looking for a mouser.

"Shreve!" my friend Gloria called one day. "You still thinking you might want a cat?"

"Yes," I said.

"Well, the O'Donnells found a litter of kittens in their barn and they're old enough now, they're looking for people that might want them."

Gloria worked at the library where most of the town news and gossip passed through.

"I told Terry you were thinking of getting one," she continued. "Do you want her number?"

I loved how quickly and easily problems got solved and questions got answered, simply because of the number of people that tended to get involved in everything that went on in town, or at least involved in sharing the information.

I called Terry and drove out to their ranch the next day. Five kittens roamed the shade of the corrals, four black-and-white, one pale gold. "They were born in a haystack," Terry told me as we squatted in the dust and teased the kittens with long weeds. "But the mother is gone, and three of the kittens have disappeared already. Either killed on the road or by coyotes," she said with a knowing shake of her head. The black kittens were friendly and affectionate, but I knew at first sight and without doubt that the scrawny yellow kitten that kept to the edges was meant to be with me. He was hard to catch and I almost gave up, almost took home a black one, but after one last scramble under the August sun, I had him in my arms, and with profuse thanks to Terry, we were off.

It was not until I had a nervous kitten roaming the inside of my truck that I realized in my excitement to fulfill my wish for a mouser, I hadn't prepared for a cat. I didn't have a litter box; I didn't have kitten food. Gloria lived halfway between my house and the O'Donnell ranch, and she and her family had six dogs and two cats. Her niece Paula, whom she and her husband were raising, had recently gotten a kitten. I swung into her driveway and dashed in, leaving the bewildered kitten in my truck with the windows cracked.

"Gloria, I just picked up a kitten from Terry's—" I blurted from her doorway.

"That's great!" she interrupted, walking up from the living room, inviting me in.

"Yes . . . but I don't have anything," I said, horrified at myself. "No litter box, no food . . . Do you have anything I can borrow until I get to town?"

" 'Course!" she sang, and I left her house generously laden with cat box, litter, and food.

Eli and I became tight overnight. We had matching demeanors and easily allowed each other's fluctuations between affection and independence. I made a harness out of thin rope that Eli wore on our first trips outside together; I wanted to be sure he became familiar with the immediate area before roaming wide and free. Eli grew into the quintessential tough guy with a heart of gold. He often came home scratched and scarred, but was devoted to me and unconditional with his love, and helped me to learn what it meant to take care of something other than myself. When Mike brought the coyote pup to my cabin door, Eli was not yet a year old; we had been together for about eight months.

Now, with the coyote in front of me, the only thing I was certain of was that I did not want fleas in my cabin. I did not want them in my bed, I did not want them on my cat, I did not want them crawling around on me. I took my eyes off the coyote to look at Mike.

"Will you take him up to your house for now? I can't let Eli get fleas."

"OK," he said.

"OK. I'll come up in an hour or so."

I walked to Mike's house and found Mike sitting at the kitchen counter. A cardboard box sat on the floor at the edge of the kitchen with the coyote curled up in the bottom of it, nestled in a bath towel.

"I sprayed him with flea spray," Mike said, looking at me. "I covered his face, though, with my hand, so he wouldn't breathe it." I remained unusually silent; my thoughts were still uncrystallized and words seemed pointless. I filled a small bowl with water and set it on the floor beside the box. I brought the coyote out of the box, still cushioned in the towel, and arranged him gently on the floor. I stretched out on the floor beside him, balanced on my hip with my head resting in my palm.

Huge, translucent fleas burrowed across the pup's round body. Methodically, I pierced them between my fingernails, one by one. I plucked them from his head and face, from behind his ears, from tunneling through the short, fine hairs of his snout. It was a repulsive task, though satisfying to see the number of industrious fleas diminishing from the coyote's fur and piling up in the dish just under the surface of the water.

As I pulled fleas from the coyote pup, I rubbed his little body. "How old is he?" I asked Mike. "About ten days," Mike said. "That's right around when they open their eyes." The pup's eyes were closed much of the time; when he opened them slightly, I saw they were a blurry, milky blue. He did not move much, and he never tried to get up. Instead, the coyote rolled onto his back and splayed his legs, entering an ecstatic state when I rubbed his belly in the seam where his legs met his body. He couldn't get enough; his front paws curled up side by side on his little gray chest, and his head tilted back in a slight arch of delight.

I had brought up some fresh goat's milk that I kept on hand as a treat for Eli and went through Mike's stash of syringes that he had for doctoring dogs and calves. I sifted through the bag until I found the one I wanted, a tiny glass syringe the length of my ring finger and the diameter of a pencil. I pulled off the needle and returned that to the bag, sterilized the syringe, and filled it with milk. With the coyote cradled in the towel in the crook of my arm, I dribbled milk from the syringe into his mouth, which was too small to take a baby bottle. After drinking what seemed to be an adequate amount, he lost interest in the syringe, and I returned the pup to his cardboard crib, and leaned across the kitchen counter to lightly kiss Mike goodbye. I left the baby coyote at Mike's house and walked down to the cabin in the dark.

The next morning, I couldn't wait to get up to Mike's to see the coyote baby. I trotted up the packed red dirt driveway so that I was out of breath when I got there. Mike had not left for work yet. He was having an obviously slow start, fumbling around, and he looked like hell. "What's wrong with you?" I asked Mike as I knelt by the cardboard box that still sat at the edge of the kitchen. "Oh, that damn coyote," he said. "He was whimpering and bawlin' all night and I never got to sleep for the noise." The flea spray had done its work. When I peeked into the box, I didn't see one flea moving around on the pup's body. I gave him one more light spray just to be safe, covering his face as Mike had done. "We'll get out of your hair." I winked at Mike, teasing him with my cheeriness as he hunched over his coffee, and walked carefully back down to the cabin with the coyote's box held tightly against my chest.

The morning was mild and I had a low fire in the woodstove to keep the cabin cozy and comfortable, and the baby coyote and I climbed into the loft to lay against the pillows. I gazed at the soft wonder that lay sleeping in my lap. His fur was dark and woolly, variations on brown, gray, and black, streaked with longer hairs of rust and silver. The puplet was soft as velvet and smelled wild. His scent was strong, distinct, like sweet musk, like the smell of sex. His ears were minuscule triangles of fur which lay sideways alongside his head when his head was up, and fell back into tiny points when he was lying down. He had a blunt, stubby snout, round paws with shiny black paw pads soft as satin, and thin claws—black, tipped in white. Eight of his claws had a round ball attached to the tip and these fell off randomly over the following days. I wondered if they were protection for the mother while she had the pups inside her.

The coyote slept most of the day, and I fed him goat's milk from the syringe when he woke. As I watched the animal clinging to my chest, rising and falling with each breath I took, I knew I could not live with any decision other than caring for this tiny orphan. And in making that choice, I knew I was locked together with this unique and mysterious being. We spent a decadently simple day together; time faded, hours blurred, the outside world ceased to exist. I was at peace; I was in peace that day.

Eli came home with the lengthening shadows of late afternoon. He meowed at the door, and when I let him in he headed straight for his dish and ate. I sat cross-legged on the bed with the coyote cradled in my lap, still wrapped in the lazy daze of our day together. After eating, Eli jumped on the bed as he had done a hundred times before, ready to lick his paws and stretch and purr, and it was then he noticed the coyote for the first time. Eli stiffened immediately, frozen in the final frame of his jump onto the bed at my feet. His eyes dilated. When I moved toward him with hopes of introducing the coyote, alleviating his anxiety, and becoming a happy family, Eli was off the bed in a flash, and he hid behind the woodstove, meowing until I let him outside.

That night, I set the coyote's box on the floor beside my bed, fortified with towels and flannel pillowcases. I got in bed and turned out the light, and within minutes, the coyote began to mournfully whimper and cry from his box. He continued for the entire night. I got no sleep. Eli did not come home.

Lethargic from my sleepless night, I spent another day lounging with the baby coyote in the cabin loft. For the first time without guilt, I let my freelance projects temporarily fall by the wayside in favor of the coyote. I knew I would make up lost time later in the week, and I had no other commitments. I had, for all intents and purposes, been fired from the school two months earlier after a year of substitute teaching. Though I was still called in on immediate notice when they could not find any other sub or if the substitute they had already lined up couldn't make it into town at the last minute, I was no longer in the school with any regularity.

During my year of steady work in the school, I tended to mix life lessons in with the curriculum I was left to teach. If I was subbing for the shop teacher and he left us to do inventory, I turned it into a lesson in Zen philosophy and mindfulness; if a second-grader threw a tantrum during art class, I took him aside and spoke to him about choice, how his day could become better from that moment forward, but the choice was his. I've always believed children deserve to be introduced to self-empowering concepts early on. So it was particularly distressing to me, one winter day, to be subbing for the music teacher and have every sixth- and seventh-grade girl search me out to talk to me privately throughout the day, either alone or in pairs, about an older boy who was hurting them. Some told me stories of being pushed down and stood upon, some could barely repeat the demeaning comments he said about their heritage, some showed me bruises. But more terrible than the stories was the look in their faces as they recounted what was going on every day. Even the tough-as-nails tomboy of the bunch was badly shaken.

Just before lunchtime, one more girl came into my room, sat down next to me on a bench below the blackboard, and told me her story, and her last sentence was what rocked me. "My mom said not to say anything; that no one will do anything about it because of whose son he is." Far worse than one adolescent's bad behavior was the lesson it seemed some adults were teaching these young teenagers—that someone in a position of power, or related to power, had rights over others' well-being; that trusted rules no longer applied. During lunch, I sought out another teacher; I knew him the best and knew how invested he was in the kids. He nodded seriously as I told him what the girls had told me. "Have them put everything they told you in writing and bring it to me," he said, "and I'll take it from there."

I stopped by the school a week later and ran into three of the seventh-grade girls in the hallway. They hugged me, told me it was all no longer an issue—though as far as I know the administration had simply moved the boy out of the classes and activities he had with the girls; it appeared that the chosen solution was simply to inhibit proximity and ignore any other issues. I was told by a school official I was never to bring up the subject again. "It is dealt with, and it will not be talked about from this point forward." After that I was rarely called in to sub. Months later, I ran into the father of the sixth-grade tomboy in the coffeeshop. "You sure did make an impression on them kids," he said, and I hold his comment as one of the great compliments of my life.

Now, on my second day with the coyote, soft light filled the cabin in the early afternoon. I nestled him between two pillows and dug around under my bureau for my camera. I hadn't used my "real" camera, my SLR, for as long as I had been in Wyoming—the few pictures I had taken in the last year-and-a-half were with a cheap point-and-shoot. I located my camera, returned to my position prone against the loft pillows, returned the coyote pup to his spot on my lap, and lost myself in photographing the tiny being that clambered around my body. He was expressive from the beginning, giving me hints of the famous coyote grin, and also curling his lip in a tiny snarl. In the early evening, I set the sleeping coyote on the center of my bed and sat at my computer to process the photos I'd taken during the day.

Eli returned to the cabin, mewing tentatively, hoping, I'm sure, the tiny intruder had vacated. I let Eli in, then returned to my desk to watch how the interaction would play out. Eli walked slowly toward the bed where the coyote was asleep on the wool bedspread. He only got half-way to the bed before he froze; he had caught the scent of coyote, his pupils widened impossibly and he bolted toward the door to crouch in the small space between the woodstove and the cabin wall. I stood up so I could look Eli in the eyes. He stared back, terrified, his expression begging to be let out. "Eli, come on," I pleaded. "Don't be afraid." I bent down beside him. "That baby can hardly walk," I tried to explain to the cat. "He's one-fourth the size you are. He can't hurt you, Eli; you could kill him if you wanted to." But Eli was overwhelmed by instinct, by a consuming fear. He mewed desperately, once more, to be let outside. I was frustrated by his instincts, but more than that, I was frustrated by how my actions, to him, seemed like the greatest betrayal. He was a coyote's natural prey, and behaved as such, and dashed out the door.

Night fell, the cabin was quiet and warm, the lights low. After Eli left, the coyote continued to sleep in a tight ball in the center of my bed and I managed to get a bit of work done at my computer, looking up regularly to eye the coyote. I was exhausted from my night without sleep and soon got the cabin ready for night. I turned off my computer, filled my water jugs for the morning with the hose outside, and brought in a large log for the woodstove that would burn slowly all night—the nights were still chilly but no longer cold. I tucked the tiny coyote into the soft layers that lined the box beside my bed, turned off the lights, undressed, and melted into my sheets.

How did the little pup know when I was separating from him—separating with sleep? He was quiet and peaceful while I spent the evening at my desk across the cabin from him, happy to sleep in a ball unto himself in the center of my bed. But less than ten minutes in the dark, just as I was drifting into a delicious sleep, the coyote began to whimper, a high, hiccuping howl; the sound of loneliness. It was constant, and I lay there in the dark thinking, *No, no . . .* , pondering how such a tiny being could make so much noise, such a desperate, unignorable noise. I couldn't bear another night like the last, so I reached down and fumbled with a blind hand until I felt warm fur. I scooped up the pup and drew him into my chest against my bare skin. He arranged himself in the shelter of my body and his cries ceased, his breathing calmed and evened, and he slept. I didn't. I was too terrified of rolling over and crushing the baby animal. Once again, the night was long and I was awake for all of it. Occasionally, the coyote stirred and I reached for the syringe I left on the steamer trunk I used as a bedside table and offered him milk; he messily drank a few mouthfuls and then fell back to sleep against my ribs.

I slid out of bed as a pastel dawn streaked the sky, slid my feet into moccasins, made coffee in the quiet of the morning. The only sounds were the cows mooing to their calves and the calves' high bleats in return. I pushed open the door to let the sunlight enter my cabin, and the morning was warm. I stood in the doorway with my back against the jamb, sipping my Folgers and honey and watching the coyote on my bed. His ears pointed sideways as he woke slowly and awkwardly. His eyes blinked clearer and clearer; they were still a pale blue but it seemed he was beginning to register his sight and notice his surroundings, taking it in. He stood on the mattress, wobbly on four chunky legs, and sniffed the sheets that rose in a pile beside him where I had pushed them aside when I got up. He took a few crooked steps and sniffed at the pillows.

Standing, he was still shorter than the thickness of a pillow. I watched him closely, amused, but ready to dash over should he wander toward the edge of the bed. But he sat again, in a perfect doglike sitting pose, and turned his head lazily from side to side, a tiny, sweet smile lighting his face. He slowed me down with his absolute adorableness.

Our day was relaxed and hazy. I was delirious after two straight nights without sleep. The coyote and I lazed around in the cabin, resting and entertaining each other simply, just being together, easy, prone. With my fingers in the coyote's fur I noticed just how dirty he was; dirt coated the skin beneath his fur, not unusual considering his first days of life were spent in a hole in the ground. I carefully packed the coyote into his box and carried it up the hill to Mike's house. His bathroom sink would make for an easier bath than heating hose water in the cabin and bathing the coyote in a mixing bowl. I let myself into Mike's empty house and closed the coyote and myself in the bathroom so he could toddle around my feet as I half-filled the sink with lukewarm water. I tested the temperature on the inside of my wrist, then scooped the coyote up from the floor and gently lowered him into the water.

The water in the sink turned dark and ruddy as dirt released from the coyote's body. I met with no resistance; he sat in the sink and leaned against my hand that supported his back, smiling in an easygoing, baby kind of way. I emptied and refilled the sink twice for clean water, lathered him lightly with my mild herbal shampoo, then cupped water in my hand to rinse the suds from him. I swaddled him in a towel and sat on the floor with the coyote on my lap and rubbed him lightly, softly.

Mike came home as I was drying off the coyote. After listening to me recount the details of the bath and, while doing so, referring to the coyote only as "the coyote," Mike asked,

"What are you going to name him?"

I don't like coming up with names or titles and find it extremely difficult. I was sure Eli had named himself and I just picked up on it telepathically.

"I have no idea," I said, resigned to my ineptitude in this arena. "I can't think of anything."

I looked up at him. "Do you want to name him?" I asked.

"Well . . . ," said Mike. He pretended to think for a moment, though I could tell he already had a name picked out.

"What about Charlie?"

I knew Charlie was the code name the government employees used when they talked about coyotes over the radio or when they were shooting from the plane in order to avoid offending anyone who might pick up the radio transmission.

"You know," said Mike. "This is 'the Charlie that got away . . .' "

"Charlie," I mused. It was undeniable—the name matched what I had already seen of his personality.

"He is a Charlie," I said, looking at Mike with a grin.

This Charlie, who represented all Charlies. It was significant.

And he was named.

Charlie's survival, at least in the short term, depended entirely on me—not one wildlife rehabilitation facility in the state took in wild canines. The overarching attitude seemed to be that since coyotes populated the area in such great number already, and were considered a nuisance anyway, it was easier, as well as bound by common sense, to kill the wounded and the orphaned; an individual coyote didn't make a difference.

While Charlie's life hinged upon me, my success hinged on learning as much as I possibly could. I knew nothing about coyotes and had never even raised a puppy. I never pretended to know what I was doing, and that gave me the great ability to learn. Mike knew volumes about coyotes, their behaviors and physiology and psychology, from a lifetime spent among them, tracking them and trapping them, learning their habits and ways. Knowing I had his experience and expertise to call upon was essential for me to feel comfortable with what I was taking on. But I needed more.

I spoke with the few people I knew who worked with wildlife and watched a sad and curious pattern of animosity unfold before me. Biologists, zoo employees, and freelance individuals that either worked with or rehabbed wild animals responded to me with an across-the-board derision. "This will end in heartbreak," they said, and, "This is not a Disney movie." They laid their words before me with the flourish of their authority. I wondered what alternative they would have wished for. Charlie's death, before he had a chance to live? What irked me was that these were people who knew me—did they honestly believe I didn't know Charlie was not a cartoon? Can't every story end in heartbreak? In their responses, they relentlessly ignored the possibility of a positive outcome; I could only guess it was because I did not have the proper background. Whether they realized it or not, they were doubting possibility, and the unknown. They believed I would fail. And when we only believe what has been said before, what has been done before, we give our own power away. Possibility evaporates; potential melts and seeps away deep into the earth below us. We cut ourselves short by thinking this way. I have always felt that it is from what we believe that our lives are created, not the other way around.

And so my days were filled with learning on my own and I spent hours in research on the internet. The most interesting articles, to me, were those on dog psychology and dog-to-dog behavior. I knew I needed to establish my dominance in Charlie's eyes from the beginning, both for my safety and for Eli's, and I wanted to know what Charlie would innately respond to, how he would interpret my behavior, and what canine behaviors I could mimic to communicate more fluently with him. "Training" was less important than communication. Charlie was wild and everything ahead of us was uncharted, unforeseeable, as we ventured into our relationship, ventured into the unknown. I paid close attention to our every interaction and made note of what was successful, working intuitively and through trial and error.

Within days, Charlie had grown just enough to drink from a baby bottle. Mike and I ran to town together and I bought a baby bottle at the hardware store; then, at the grocery store, always the last stop on the list of errands, I went down the baby aisle and saw a cuter bottle and bought that one too.

"Has the readerboard changed?" I asked Mike as we approached the turn near the Methodist church on our way home. I had hardly left the cabin since Charlie entered it.

"Mmm, don't know," said Mike. He didn't comprehend nor appreciate my fascination with the sign, but he slowed for me as we passed it: "*1+X is greater than 1+0,*" it read.

"OK, do you see why I love it?" I asked him, laughing. "God and algebra! I'm tempted to go to a service just to meet the mind behind the sign." I glanced over at Mike, he was shaking his head and smiling.

Mike dropped me and my groceries off at the cabin; I left the bags on the counter and filled the bottles with milk, eager to try them out. Charlie relaxed against my arm and happily drank from the bottles. He looked up at me as milk dribbled out the side of his mouth and I smiled back down at him. He did not suck very well, and I cut the opening in the nipples slightly larger, so that he could get milk easily without choking on too much. He liked to gnaw the nipple rhythmically between his back teeth to bring the milk out.

A week later, as Charlie was grinding the nipple in his back teeth the way he always did, milk began gushing out, all over Charlie and all over my lap. Charlie had chewed the tip completely off the nipple. Frantically, I fished around his mouth with my finger but he had swallowed it. I called Mike in tears, convinced Charlie would die from the nipple becoming lodged in his intestinal tract. "Stop worrying," Mike said gently. "Coyotes are tough. They can eat a tin can and shit out a nail." I trusted Mike, but kept an eye on Charlie. It took two weeks to see the nipple again. From then on, Charlie drank from a dish, and for some odd, unexplainable reason, he always stood with one of his front paws in the bowl of milk while he lapped it up.

Charlie quickly learned how to climb out of his small box and I found a tall cardboard box that was roughly three feet cubed. I made a nest in the bottom with towels and sweatshirts that I first slept in to imbue them with my scent. This functioned as Charlie's crate; I put Charlie in the box when I left the cabin and draped a towel over the top to darken it. While he still slept a great deal, Charlie was active and curious when he awoke, and scuttled around the cabin exploring every crevice and crack, falling over my shoes, chasing stray feathers from the duvet. I barricaded the space under my bed with sheets and pillows so Charlie could not get lost or into mischief, and with that one area blockaded, Charlie was able to roam the small cabin freely. He loved being on the bed and exerted himself to no end trying to climb straight up the side, clawing his way up the bedspread and heaving himself over the crest of the mattress to finally rest on the bed. I placed a small needlepoint stool I inherited from a great-aunt next to the steamer trunk I used as a bedside table, then layered small pillows to form a ramp from the trunk to the height of the mattress. After showing him these new "stairs" once, Charlie hopped up on the little stool, then onto the chest, and then climbed the pillows to reach the bed. Once up, he was stuck. No matter how many times I helped him down the ramp of pillows, he never went down that way; instead, he stood at the edge, and peered forlornly over the side until I scooped him up and deposited him on the floor. Sometimes, Charlie climbed up onto the stool, stopped there, and sat comfortably on his haunches, elegant even as a toddler, watching everything.

The weather was changing, warming toward summer. Lilacs bloomed throughout the town, their scent mixing with dust and sage in the warm air. After keeping a fire lit all day and night for so many months, it felt strange to stop; it was something I mourned. With no fire in the wood-stove, I used an electric hotplate to heat water in the morning for coffee and to wash my face. I was convinced the coffee did not taste as good when made with water heated on a burner. But losing the fire brought the gain of running water, and I took showers outside in the lean-to be-hind the cabin and dried just by sitting in the sun. I was taking photos of Charlie every day, documenting the miracle that had landed in my life, watching the wonder unfolding, and through Charlie, rekindled my love for photography. I began emailing my photos of Charlie to friends and extended family, just one photo at a time, and when I real-ized I had been sending pictures every single day, I facetiously titled the email "Your Daily Coyote." The name and the concept stuck, and I con-tinued to email a daily photo after my grandmother, cousins, and city friends made it clear that they could no longer begin their day without their picture of Charlie.

Eli began to spend more time in the cabin but he spent it in the loft, where he knew he was out of reach of the coyote. I sent out the wish, daily, that Eli would let go of his fear and start to behave in such a way that Charlie would see Eli as a leader, and that maybe, that would keep Charlie from ever becoming a threat to Eli. When Eli did venture down from the loft to eat or to leave, Charlie galloped over to him with his tiny tail wagging, eager for acceptance and friendship. Eli was conflicted. He no longer ran away from Charlie, but when Charlie approached with a face full of grins, Eli stopped, midstride, his eyes thin slits of irritation, and gave Charlie a glare that said, *What are you doing in my house, taking attention away from me. I hate you.* Charlie was always determined to play, and desperate to befriend the cat with a touch, a nuzzle, or a lick, but if he persisted too long, Eli gave him a quick swat across the head and Charlie whimpered away, and sat nearby looking over his shoulder like he was waiting for Eli's approval. Which he never got.

I took Charlie with me up to Mike's a few times, but Charlie did not like it; he seemed overwhelmed by the huge space and disturbed by the noise of the TV or radio, one of which was always on. When let to wander, Charlie went straight to the laundry room and hid behind the dryer. And so, Charlie and I spent our time in and around the cabin. I still had the little rope harness I had made for Eli as a kitten, and with a few alterations of the knots, I could slip it easily around Charlie's chest and neck. When he was around four weeks old, I carried him outside and sat under the trees beside the cabin with Charlie on my lap, the harness already on him, unsure what his reaction to the outdoors would be or what he would be inspired to do. Charlie was content to stay in my lap for quite a while, with his nose raised to the warm May breeze. Birds caught his attention both visually and aurally, and soon, he gathered himself up and hopped off my legs to sniff delicately and tentatively in

the tall grass at the base of the tree trunks. I held on to the end of the rope, though it proved to be unnecessary. Charlie did not wander far nor fast, and soon became exhausted. I made a little nest for him with a quilted wool shirt, and he curled up in it with his chin on his crossed paws, alert and peaceful in the world outside the den.

Charlie continued to sleep with me every night, but I put him between the covers and the top sheet because his little claws were like talons on bare skin. His baby teeth were small and sharp and I gave him a small deer antler to teethe on. The antler became his favorite toy, and the tips of the tines became grooved with thin hatchmarks from his gnawing. He loved to pretend to kill socks and dish towels—he took them in his mouth and shook them rapidly as a grown coyote would shake a rabbit to break its neck. It was hilarious and also fascinating to watch such determined viciousness in such a tiny being—yet Charlie knew the difference between his toys and my body. Whenever we played or tussled, he never clamped down on me. He did test his jaw strength on my hands or arm, a natural stage in a puppy's growth, one that is usually monitored and conditioned by the mother or more dominant littermates. The moment Charlie began to bite with greater pressure, I would say "Gentle" in a low, firm voice and bite him on his ear, as canine mothers often do with their pups. He soon learned the meaning of the word "gentle," and all I needed to do was say it, without biting his ear, and he immediately lightened the pressure of his bite and even mouthed the air around my hand without touching me at all to show he understood.

Charlie loved having his belly rubbed where his back legs met his body, so much so, I thought he had a skin condition. I slathered lotion and anti-itch cream on the area, but came to realize it was just his thing, his spot, his comfort. He would waddle over to me and tip sideways into me to show me his belly and that it needed to be rubbed. If that didn't work, he wrapped his front paws around my wrist and dragged my hand under his body.

Housebreaking was an effort, largely because I didn't have a protected yard to just let him out in and I really didn't know what I was doing. I rolled up my rugs, stocked up on baby wipes to clean messes from my plywood floor, and put Eli's litter box in plain view. Charlie did pee on the floor, but in the beginning I didn't care as much as I probably should have. The puddles were incredibly small, the odor was incredibly mild, and it was coyote pee on my floor. It was so exotic. Yet as Charlie grew, so did his puddles, and it was no longer novel or charming. I realized then I should have been training him from day one, but eventually, I got him using the cat's litter box.

In late May, I heard Mike's dogs bark in wild unison as his truck neared the driveway and crossed the cattle guard. His truck engine grew louder as he approached the cabin, then it idled and stopped. I heard his footsteps on my porch, his knock at the door. This was our ritual; on his way home, Mike often stopped at the cabin to visit and chat; now he stopped to see Charlie, too.

I flicked the hook-and-eye latch on my door—I had no doorknob—and pushed open the door for Mike to enter. He was silhouetted against the afternoon sun as he stepped into the cabin and I was blinded for a moment as my eyes adjusted back from the flash of daylight. Even in the cabin, Mike's pupils were tight pinpricks; I never saw them change with the changing light. As we fell into a hug, Charlie waddled at speed to where Mike stood, sniffed his tennis shoes, chewed playfully at the hem of his Wranglers.

"Chuck!" Mike stooped down. "Hey there, Chuck."

His hands covered Charlie's body.

Charlie loved Mike's attention, fell back against Mike's ankle and onto the floor, rolling over on his back, all four paws curled in glee. Mike laughed a quiet, unassuming laugh, a laugh that was more to himself than in the world. He shook his head in wonderment as Charlie writhed on the floor like a fish, still shocked by this coyote's open adoration, though the same choreography between them occurred every few days, whenever Mike stopped by the cabin.

Today, I was filled with relief to see Mike, to see the cuffs of his shirtsleeves snapped modestly around his heavy wrists, to see his skin emerging from the crisp sleeves, dark-tanned already from so much time spent outside. On the days he flew I never fully relaxed. Since moving to Wyoming, I'd heard too many stories of my friends losing family members when these small, fixed-wing planes crashed in the mountains. Gloria's father died this way, en route to a remote welding assignment, as did my landlady's uncle, flying the mountain looking for lost sheep. Mike had already walked away from two crash landings while gunning from government planes.

"I'm not gonna crash," he had said to me more times than I could count. "Plus," he told me early in our relationship, "I get hazard pay when I fly." Mike was putting his daughter through college.

"How much is hazard pay?" I asked.

"Thirty bucks a day."

Which seemed like more of an insult than compensation. "I'll pay you thirty bucks not to fly," I had said, only half joking.

But today, while Charlie scrambled around his hand, Mike was the one unloading the frustrations that were building with his job.

The budget of Mike's department had recently, through state funding, been significantly increased and Mike was spending his days training the new men his bosses had hired, in addition to doing his own job. Mike took the new hires as a blow after having taken care of the county alone for close to twenty years. Mike used his job the way some people use alcohol—to keep himself from feeling.

The new money was spent on new trucks for the new hires and funded additional pilots and planes stationed around the state. Mike was gunning from the plane more than he ever had, more than he needed to. "It doesn't even take skill to do this job anymore." Mike lamented. "Anyone can kill coyotes from an airplane."

But none could kill as well as Mike. The average, shooting from the plane, was two dead coyotes per hour. Mike, being a ruthless shot and having an uncanny ability to see coyotes from the sky that consistently surprised the pilots he flew with, could often average five an hour. When he flew, it was not uncommon for Mike to kill between twenty and thirty coyotes in one day.

Our conversation woke Eli who had been sleeping in the loft, and he came tripping down the ladder, ignored us, and went straight for his food dish. Charlie turned in an awkward semicircle to gallop after the cat. At six weeks old, Charlie's legs were lengthening but he had no grace whatsoever, at which Eli blatantly scoffed—one time, Charlie stuck his entire head into a tennis shoe and I actually saw the cat roll his eyes. Now, Charlie joined Eli in the kitchen corner. Charlie was still small enough to walk under the cat between Eli's legs, and did. Eli stood there astounded, with an expression of horror, yet dynamics between the two were improving daily. Eli grew out of his fear into tolerance, the tolerance of a much older brother who had resigned to his weary fate as the recipient of Charlie's shameless adoration. They ate side by side, and Eli even allowed Charlie to crawl around on him, as long as Eli was half asleep.

Charlie's head popped out from around Mike's calf. He was getting pointy; his nose, his ears, even his paws drew out into exaggerated angles. "Charlie," I cooed to him, "your ears get larger daily." I pointed out to Mike the changes that were taking place: the lightening of his muzzle, the black half-diamond markings that were coming in under his eyes like a football player's, the thin black stripes running down his forelegs. And though in the face he looked like a mini coyote, his tail was still thin and rather rat-like, and he still fit in my cupped hands, still waddled around with a little baby body, and from above he looked like an eggplant.

Evening was coming on, and Mike never stayed too long at the cabin. I had always been willing to go up to his house, and that was where we always spent our time together; he had never spent a night in the cabin with me. Now with Charlie in the picture, we saw each other frequently, but with less regularity, for shorter durations. I had left Charlie in his box once and gone up to stay the night with Mike, but after a few restless hours in his bed, watching the heat lightning filling the sky to the north and east, I slipped out in the dark, and drove back to the cabin in the middle of the night with my underwear in my pocket. I slipped into bed with the coyote, and hadn't spent a night away from the cabin since.

My phone rang at six the next morning. "Hey Shreve," said Joslyn, one of my favorite friends, in her singsong voice. Joslyn had grown up in Ten Sleep and worked for one of the largest sheep ranchers in the area.

"I wanted to see if you wanted to come feed lambs with me," she asked.

We made plans to meet at the corner of town and drive out to the lamb shed together. I quickly fed Charlie, nestled him in his cardboard crate, and draped a towel over the top, then threw on jeans and a sweatshirt and headed out. The dawn was soft and calm, the light gentle across the sky, the air warm. Joslyn was waiting for me at the designated corner, and I parked my truck and jumped into her pickup. Joslyn was twenty-one and a beauty even at dawn, with freckles covering perfectly proportionate features and thick, wavy auburn hair falling wildly half-way down her back. We were dressed nearly identically in dirty jeans, sweatshirts, and cowboy boots, and we spent the drive catching up in easy conversation; it had been a few weeks since we had seen each other. She drove us just out of town, down a curving dirt road lined with cottonwoods that ran alongside one of the few creeks, out through a field to a maze of weatherworn stables and corrals. Lambs that were orphaned or ignored by their mothers were under her charge and had to be fed by hand. Two dozen of these young, gangly lambs greeted us, bleating and hopping around our legs when we stepped over the rail fence into their pen. They were eager, and knew they were about to be fed. Their faces were warm as they butted against my thigh while we made our way through the cloud of lambs and into a dim stable. The corrals had been built many decades earlier; they seemed to stay erect only by a precarious balance. The boards were gray, ancient, the lines uneven, no true horizontals anywhere. A glimmering pattern of shadow and light played on the dirt floor inside the shed from the morning light beaming in through the cracks.

Joslyn grabbed two large buckets and we squeezed through a rough stable door at the opposite side of the shed, careful not to let any of the lambs out, tromped through weeds and ducked underneath broken-down rail fences to a water spigot set deep in the network of corrals. We filled the buckets and each carried one as carefully as possible, water inevitably sloshing over the sides of the buckets and splashing our jeans as we navigated the obstacle course back to the shed and the lambs. There, Joslyn mixed powdered milk replacer into the water. She dipped an old metal coffee can into one of the buckets, the rim of the can bent crudely to form a spout, and filled clean beer bottles with the sticky, sweet milk replacer, then fitted the bottles with long black nipples.

Joslyn scooped up a lamb and held it in one arm against her hip, with the bottle tilted for the lamb in her other hand.

"Just grab one," she said to me. "They just want to eat, they'll let you. Just hold it on your hip, kind of—it's easy if you put your foot up on the rail . . . just let their legs hang. They don't care!"

I scooped up a lamb, holding it tightly against my body with its weight resting on my cocked hip. Its body was dense and warm, spongy from a layer of young wool. The lamb dove its head straight for the bottle I was holding and sucked vigorously on the nipple, gulping milk. I looked over at Joslyn and laughed at the sight of her with her lamb; the lamb was so focused on drinking, delighting in it, its four long legs dangling in the air. Once the lamb drank a bottle's worth, Joslyn bent and let it go, grabbed another beer bottle, and scooped up another lamb.

The lambs were different ages and sizes, and all different colors—some were cream, black, or chocolate brown; a few had white bodies and tan or gray speckled legs and faces. Joslyn kept track by sight which lambs had been fed and which still needed to be, and I asked her to point out which one to go for before I grabbed one; I could not distinguish them individually except by color.

We talked little, as we fed each lamb one by one, but enjoyed each other's company in the dusky light of the barn, surrounded by the silence of the morning. This was her life, her routine. Regardless of what else went on in her day, every morning and evening she drove out here alone and fed the eager lambs one at a time.

"Do you ever get lonely?" I asked her, suddenly.

She looked up, obviously surprised. I couldn't tell if she was surprised by the intimacy of the question, or surprised at the concept of being lonely.

"I don't think so," she answered with a small smile, and went back to feeding her lamb.

We finished up, collected the bottles, and poured some feed in long, low troughs that the older lambs ate as a supplement. The lambs continued to bound around us, and they drew my fingers into their cavernous mouths, sucking hard, hoping for more milk. I could feel the ridges of the roof of each lamb's mouth on the pad of my finger and the soft pressure of its tongue below.

"Do you want a lamb?" Joslyn asked me as we were about to leave. "You can have one," she said excitedly. "You can take it home, and feed it just like we did today, and raise it . . . If you want?"

I forced a smile, suppressing the monumental sigh that filled me inside. How could I say, "I'd love that, but I actually have a coyote living in my cabin?" How could I tell her, the granddaughter of sheep and cattle ranchers and the hired hand of another respected sheep rancher, that I was harboring the enemy?

"Maybe," I said lamely. "I'm so busy right now . . . can I think about it?"

I so badly wanted to tell her the truth, that I had my hands full already raising a baby coyote, but I couldn't. Coyotes are shot on sight, both for sport and because it has been ingrained through generations that coyotes are a threat to livestock and therefore to livelihood. I wasn't ready for the town, or anyone in it, to know about Charlie just yet. And though I was simply keeping the truth secret from Joslyn, it felt like I was lying to her about myself.

That night, the full moon was spectacular. I got up at four a.m. and slipped outside to sit on the dusty boards of my porch and simply gaze at the moonlight because it was so beautiful. Eight deer tiptoed through the sagebrush below the cabin. They watched me watching them as they grazed; then, in one swift movement, they bounded up the draw and over the hill. As morning drew near, the moon grew larger and larger as it edged toward the horizon, becoming huge and golden as it set and the sun rose.

I stepped back into the cabin and Charlie was awake. He wagged his tail as I walked toward him. I stooped down to him and he reached up to me and covered my face with the softest, most deliberate little licks. I had no idea how much time I had with this precious animal. If, as he grew, it became clear that the best thing for Charlie would be for him to be wild and free, I would never keep him for myself. I would resist interfering with human logic or my own desires, and assumed I would take him into the wild—Mike knew of two nearby areas that would provide a relatively safe environment for Charlie to live out his life—when he was around six months old. Though I knew there was some chance that Charlie could become permanent family, I found it highly unlikely. And so I savored every moment, every soft coyote kiss.

Three

June

Dawn nudged me from sleep around five, as it did every morning now, with sun and bright warmth flooding my windows. Summer is a time of light in Wyoming, the skies brighten at four and darkness does not approach until after ten. Charlie was still asleep at my neck, curled into a comma with his nose and paws tucked around his body; his long, thin tail flung to the side betraying the perfect roundness of his form. I turned my head and nuzzled my face into the fur of his flank. The instant he felt me stirring deliberately, his head popped up and his eyes smiled at me and he stretched his pointy face toward mine to lick me good morning.

At two months, Charlie slept soundly for as long as I did, and the moment I awoke, he did too. He stood up on the bed and took a deep stretch into an enviable downward dog and yawned, still resting on his elbows. His tongue rolled into a long, sweeping curl just inside his gaping mouth, adding a comical element to the formidable sight of a jaw that, I estimated, opened into an outrageous 130-degree angle. Baby teeth glinted from within and they were sharp and serrated, the Tetons in miniature. After luxuriating in his stretch, Charlie wagged his tail twice in a happy wiggle and pranced onto my chest, licking my own jawline and my lips. I rubbed his body and noted how much he was growing, and so quickly. I sat up, carrying him on my chest with me, and set him on the floor as I got out of bed; he still jumped straight off the bed onto the plywood floor instead of taking the stairs, and was small enough for the jump to seem dangerous.

Charlie raced across the cabin and dove onto a toy mouse lying near the woodstove as I put water on for tea and reached for a pair of dirty jeans I had left hanging on a nail near the door the day before. I had a box of nails in my kitchen cupboard and dipped into it often—whenever I needed hooks, whether to organize my coffee mugs on the kitchen wall, to drape with scarves in the winter, or to hang damp jeans to dry in the summer, I pounded a long nail into a log. Instant utility, and, since the cabin was so rustic, the raw nails blended into the ambience without looking tacky. Or else I had gotten so hillbilly I didn't care. My jeans were dry and I pulled them on, then threw on a loose gray t-shirt streaked with stains of red mud across the front. Charlie ran in manic arcs around the cabin floor with the stuffed mouse clamped proudly in his jaw, stopping short to spit out the mouse and drink a few laps of water, to take a pit stop in the litter box, to devour a few mouthfuls of meat, to spin on his heel and go after a small, weather-bleached vertebrae bone, one of his favorite toys, that lay half obscured in the shadows under my desk. I sipped my tea and sat cross-legged on the floor to roughhouse with him, dragging a dish towel in circles around my body for him to chase, rolling him on his back and rubbing him down.

Charlie stopped mid-run at the faintest sound on the wooden boards outside. Moments later, Eli meowed at the door, returning from whatever it was he did in the wee hours. I barred Charlie from the door with my foot and Eli snaked in, and was immediately accosted by his coyote brother. Charlie ran clumsy circles around the cat, wagging his tail and eagerly reaching in to lick Eli's face. Eli stood for him with a weary tolerance; he hadn't asked to be anybody's idol, he hadn't asked to be anyone's friend, for that matter. When Eli felt he had humored Charlie long enough, he strode forward, knocking Charlie aside with his shoulder as he made his way to the kitchen corner to eat. Charlie darted back to where I sat on the floor putting on my socks and tumbled over my foot; such simple, raw happiness radiated from him when the three of us were together. He seemed so easily and completely thrilled by the connection of the three of us sharing a space. He tugged at the length of sock before I had it fully over my foot and nosed his skinny little snout up under my jeans as I pulled it all the way on.

The cat had reclaimed the bed in tandem with his new confidence with Charlie, and with an effortless jump, made himself comfortable on the duvet. I scooped up Charlie and set him gently in the bottom of his cardboard box. I knew he would wind down and nap happily while I left to irrigate. I was too nervous to leave Charlie outside while I was not around; anyway, we would spend much of the day outside once I returned. I grabbed my sunglasses off the counter and closed the door to the sounds of Charlie quietly scratching around in his box. Out on the porch, I pulled knee-high rubber boots up over my jeans, jumped in my truck and drove out to the fields.

I liked being in the fields before seven. That early, it was beautifully warm and faintly breezy, not too hot. Above me, the colors of

sunrise slowly faded into the delicate blue of day, and the untamed BLM rolled out behind me. This unobstructed natural land was my view while I irrigated—undulations of red dirt edged with sage, white patches of alkali, the deep, organic cuts of draws, all leading to the Bighorns which rose near the horizon, blue with juniper and distance. The colors that filled my vision were muted and unexpected, rust and dark dusty blue and golden and tan. If I turned around, I could see scattered houses behind me, and the bright green leaves of the trees that stood around these houses were incongruent in the natural color scheme; so were the small, round leaves of the alfalfa that blanketed the field in which I stood. True green didn't occur naturally; trees and alfalfa only grew with the intervention of man. Summer rains were rare and rejoiced in, and irrigating water was rationed—so precious that the saying went, "Steal a man's wife, just don't steal his water."

During the summer, ranchers took their cows and sheep up the mountain to graze while in the valley, grass and alfalfa fields were cultivated and put up as hay to be fed through the winter and spring until new grass had a chance to grow once again. Most ranchers sold off their breeding cows when they reached a certain age, a wise maneuver from a business standpoint, but Mike was oddly attached to his cows. He knew all their temperaments and personalities and kept them until they died of old age; some of his cows were eighteen and twenty years old. While he ran the majority of his cows on the mountain for the summer, he also leased two fields for what he called his "special needs" bunch. Instead of raising the alfalfa for winter hay, he put the very old and the very young in these pastures where they had lush, easy grazing all summer long, and I irrigated these fields in trade for rent.

When Mike asked me if I'd be interested in irrigatin' I said yes without knowing what irrigatin' was. Afterward, I regretted my answer and dreaded the impending commitment; I had no idea what I had consented to do. "Just laying out pipe" was all Mike said. "I'll show you next week." Irrigatin' was the ultimate workout–a combination of cardio, weights, and squats. A water hydrant stood in the center of each pasture. I ran aluminum pipe out from the hydrant, then joined more pipe in an exaggerated 'T' to run the length of the field. I had ten days of water each month for each pasture, and every day I added a new pipe to the center line and moved the rest of the pipes down, across the field, so that over the course of ten days, the row of irrigation pipes traveled the width of the field. Essentially, each bit of grass got hit with water only one day out of every month.

The metal pipes were thirty feet long. Some were three inches in diameter, some four, and they all had a riser at one end with a sprinkler head on it. It took about sixty-five pipes to run the length of the larger pasture and thirty-five for the smaller one. The pipes were heavy and awkward; balance was key in carrying them across the field. The pipes joined together with a metal latch, but they had to be precisely aligned and the slightest off-angle meant they would not lock no matter how much force I used, no matter how much I swore in the empty field. If the connection was not secure, the pressure of the water would blow the pipes apart. Irrigatin' was a time to get zen. The first time I irrigated, it took me three hours to do just the large pasture, but as I got stronger and got used to the work, learning by feel and learning from my mistakes, I got to where I could do both pastures in an hour and a half.

Once all the pipes were connected and the ends capped, I went to the hydrant and turned up the water. I could hear the pipes filling; the sprinklers at the bottom of the line began to sputter with water and slowly turn, then the noise of the pressure intensified as the line filled completely. There was a moment of silence before the sprinklers awoke, all of them down the line, like a sigh, a caught breath released, and I watched the perfect row plume into giant sprays of water that reached feet over my head. I always walked back across the fields hugging the line, making sure each sprinkler head was turning properly, and getting lightly showered by the falling drops as my reward for the work.

It was hot by the time I got back to the cabin. I left my muddy rubber boots outside; stripped off my socks and wet jeans as well. Charlie was all wiggles and sweetness when I pulled him out of his box and I slid his little harness over his head and chest and tied him to a support beam outside while I took a fast shower in the lean-to beside the cabin. I wrapped myself in a towel and stretched out on the porch to dry in the sun while Charlie pounced on bugs that hid in the weeds in front of the cabin.

Nature in her summer glory was full of stimulation as Charlie and I explored the tiny details of the world around the cabin. Together, we looked closer, listened, felt. Life was rich and magical even where it seemed barren and impossible. Tiny flowers budded upon cacti; delicate, pale grasses sprouted up through dusty red dirt; cottontails, meadowlarks, and blackbirds darted through fields and sky. Once dry, I dressed again, in a variation of my summer uniform of tank top, jeans, cowboy boots. It was hot but Charlie and I were off on our morning walkabout, to dash up draws and wander through the sagebrush, and boots and jeans were essential. Charlie understood the prep and was getting excited, hopping up onto the porch and back down again. I stooped down to gently remove his harness and left it tied to the porch.

We tripped down the draw, Charlie dancing at my heels, and set out through the tall meadow grass that was growing even faster than

Charlie was. Though he leapt away to pounce on a grasshopper or follow a scent trail around a craggy sagebrush, Charlie never strayed far
without coming back to check in, as if he knew he was allowed a certain
diameter to explore. A tamarisk tree was leafing out and Charlie ran to
its complicated base–instead of a proper trunk, it was as if a mass of
branches grew straight out of the ground. Charlie scratched around in
the dirt. "Charlie!" I said, and his little head popped up from the tangle
of branches to look at me. "Come," I said, as I knelt in the grass and
tapped my fingers on the ground. Charlie pranced over, and we made
our way deeper into the meadow, Charlie hopping through the arched,
graceful stalks of feathery weeds.

Eli bounded up to us in a series of great leaps, his tail held high in
a sweeping shepherd's crook. He must have been napping secretively in
the dirt behind the cabin when Charlie and I were lounging out front.
Though Eli projected an air of indifference, he often made it a point
to tag along on our walks. I had never gone on a walk with the cat. Eli
darted past us, efficient and hyperaware. He sharpened his claws on low
brush, raced at lightening speed after an invisible thing he would then
attack, all sleekness and grace. Eli stopped at intervals and checked on
Charlie, who liked to follow Eli as best he could but still fell down if
he turned around too fast. They were roughly the same size, though
Charlie weighed about half of what Eli did; Eli was all muscle and
Charlie was all head and stick legs. Eli had warmed up to his little coyote brother and even initiated contact, rubbing his body along Charlie's
the way that cats do. I had a brief paranoia that Eli's befriending Charlie
would embolden him toward other coyotes, coyotes that would eat
him, but Charlie's scent had changed. I assumed Eli knew Charlie's
particular, milder smell, and would not be suddenly accepting of all
coyotes. Eli seemed to understand his role as mentor and babysitter
and came to my side when I meowed, bringing Charlie in behind him,

and Charlie began responding to a meow as well. He came when I said, "Come," and came when I said, "Kitten!"

When we returned to the cabin, I made a salad while Eli tormented Charlie from the third step of the ladder to the loft, just out of Charlie's reach. Eli crouched on the step, reached his front paw long and low and quickly whapped Charlie across the ear, then immediately sat back up in a priestly pose while Charlie ran circles below him, desperately trying to calculate how he might reach the cat. Just as Charlie lost hope and turned away in resignation, Eli reached down again to bat Charlie once more, and the game—or torment—continued on. Though entertaining, I couldn't completely support Eli's sadistic pleasure in taunting Charlie. I tossed Charlie half a carrot—he ate nearly everything I gave him to try. Charlie pounced on the length of carrot and pretended to attack it, then gnawed ferociously on one end before actually tasting a sample, and then he ate it up. After I told Mike stories of Charlie feasting on various vegetables, he pretended to be horrified that I had turned Charlie into a vegetarian, which in Ten Sleep was an insult on par with calling someone a Republican in Santa Cruz. I countered that if Charlie was a vegetarian, then no one would worry about him killing sheep.

Though Charlie loved vegetables, he loved meat more. His main staple was elk, and Mike had a freezer full of elk that had been stockpiled from years of hunting—some of it was several years old, and that I cooked for Charlie. On my daily trips to the chest freezer down at the corrals, I'd involuntarily jump as the freezer was usually filled with tiny frozen bats and severed skunk heads that Mike collected for his job and sent in to test for rabies.

Mike called as the buttes darkened and a ruby sunset spread across the sky.

"Can I take you to town and buy you a real dinner?" he asked.

"You're on," I said.

"I'll pick you up in five minutes," he said, which meant he was on his way down, and I ran to find shoes and wrangle Charlie into his box. With a few quick sweeps I had my hair up and mascara on. There was only one little restaurant in town, but Mike and I still treated these weekly outings like dates. From the open doorway, I saw his truck navigate the sloping, winding dirt road on its way to my cabin, cresting a rise here, turning there as it kept its path toward me. Sometimes, there is no better sight. It's the sight of anticipation, of the country with mountains as a backdrop and horse pastures flanking the drive; it's the sight of excitement, of this man arriving to see me, that I may see his eyes and the tilt of his head as he smiles at me from his pickup. I latched the cabin door closed and jumped in his truck, meeting his smile.

"Man, you are easy on the eyes," he said with a shake of his head.

"You look good yourself," I said with a grin. His blue eyes were set off by a clean, bright turquoise button-up shirt.

"Yeah, I washed the grime off." He laughed and grabbed my hand, and held it all the way to town.

The café was about half filled, a few families, a couple of old bachelor cowboys. We took a table in the corner and the waitress brought us drinks, iced tea for me, a Pepsi for Mike; she knew our standard order.

"You're getting a steak, aren't you?" Mike asked across the small table.

"Yes," I said, acting like he was twisting my arm. It was our standard script.

"So what went on with you today?" I asked.

Mike clouded up. "Oh, the damn cows got out, my phone was full of messages with people complaining about it, but I was flying and couldn't do anything about it till afternoon—one of these new hires isn't certified to gun from the plane." He stretched his hand and made a fist and stretched it again. "And that pilot banks the plane right over the coyotes instead of flying alongside them running, so I have to shoot down and my hand takes the recoil of the shotgun instead of my shoulder; this knuckle just took a beating, I can barely button my jeans. And the neighbor borrowed my backhoe and didn't even put gas in it and these damn gas prices keep going up, and wages don't go up to match it . . ."

None of this was new. He'd been used by his neighbor before; he'd flown with that pilot multiple times and instead of asking the pilot to bank differently, he shot from a place of pain; the cows regularly knocked the hose out of their water tank in one pasture—an easy fix with a bit of wire and a rock—but when the cows drained the tank, they went elsewhere in search of water. I couldn't feel sorry for him, because I believed all the problems were fixable. But I hated hearing his frustration, hated the damper it brought on his mood and our time together.

"Maybe," I ventured, "you want all these problems to happen. There's always something, it seems, and if you have to deal with whatever it is, you don't have any time left over," my voice softened, "to deal with Tracy." He was watching me, half curious, half skeptical, so I kept going. "Maybe you actually want these things to happen and bring them into your life because they keep you occupied."

"But I don't want these things to happen," he said.

We were speaking two different languages. I tried a different tack.

"Maybe the reason your life seems filled with bad experiences and ungrateful people is because after what happened, you decided—and truly believe—the world is a horrible place, and that all these experiences are coming to you to affirm and reinforce your belief. They're showing you that what you believe is right! And maybe a way to begin to alter that, to keep this pattern from continuing on, is to change your belief about the world—but to do that you would have to come to a different understanding of Tracy's death, and I don't know if that is possible. But maybe a way to begin would be to acknowledge—and really acknowledge—one good thing in the world every day."

Mike laughed quietly and shook his head. "I don't think you know how difficult that will be for me."

I wanted him to find peace more than anything, but Mike and I had very different opinions of death, and very different experiences with it. I didn't see death as a bad thing, and didn't see it as an ending—it was life that was hard and full of pain. It was not until I was about twenty-five that the days I didn't want to die outnumbered the days I did. I don't know if it was from going gluten-free or from doing enough soul searching and internal work that I finally was able to turn things around and now, it was hard for me to remember how dark I had been.

"What's one good thing that happened in your life today?"

"Ummm . . ." he sighed, and looked off toward the corner where the wall met the ceiling. Silence. Then his face lightened. "I'm having dinner with you!"

I laughed; not quite the answer I was going for, but there it was.

"You'll never guess what Charlie did today," I said. "He climbed the ladder to the loft!"

"You're kiddin' me," Mike said.

"He did. He's seen Eli go up and down a million times, and today, he just started on up and climbed all the way to the top! I had to carry him down, I didn't want him to go headfirst into the floor, but can you believe that?"

"Unbelievable. That's like a straight-up ladder—my dogs won't even go up the log staircase in the house."

We laughed about Charlie throughout dinner, and when we finished, we wrapped our steak trimmings in layers of paper napkins, waved our goodbyes to the kitchen, and went out into the night.

Mike pulled up in front of the cabin and I reached over to hug him. "Want to come in?" I asked.

Mike nodded against my shoulder. "I gotta see how Charlie likes his steak," he said. "And I really want to see your latest pictures."

Charlie welcomed us with wiggles and licks and clambered all over Mike while I cut the scraps of fat into small pieces. The aroma of steak drew Charlie over to where I stood, and he reached his paws up the leg of my jeans as far as he could reach. I handed him a small bit of fat which he eagerly took in his mouth. He made slow, deliberate circles around the front of the cabin, hugging the walls. Mike and I sat on our heels, leaning against the kitchen cupboard, giggling quietly as Charlie squirmed between one of my cowboy boots and the cabin wall, hid the piece of fat in the crevice, and then diligently covered it with imaginary dirt. Charlie held an expression of absolute seriousness and focus as he pawed the ground and then nosed the space around his hidden morsel as if he were shoveling dirt over it with his snout. When he emerged, I gave him another piece and we watched him repeat the scene, this time burying it behind the woodstove. Mike and I leaned against each other, laughing quietly. I tossed the rest of the bits of fat in Charlie's food dish, for him to have whenever he got hungry, and while he took them one by one and hid the pieces around the cabin, Mike and I shared my computer chair, the only chair in the cabin, and I showed him the latest photos I'd taken of Charlie.

"You're still sending out one a day?" he asked.

"Yes!" It still surprised me. "People are loving it. I was nervous they'd get fed up with me filling up their inbox with a picture every day, but I get so much email back—my grandmother has made it clear she cannot start her day without Charlie; Linda, my boss from when I was a teenager, forwards my emails on to a list of her friends; my friend Chris in New York said he shows Charlie's pictures to the models and crew of every photo shoot he works on . . . it's so funny. Charlie's got a fan club."

Mike chuckled as I scrolled through the recent pictures, commenting briefly about an expression or composition. "I can't believe you can turn this old red dirt and sage that I drive past every day into such damn good pictures." Mike's voice was soft, like running water; his words traveled softly into one another. When he talked to me, it was like being caressed; it was deliberate, fleeting, which made it erotic. We leaned together in a slow kiss. "Sure you don't want to stay?" I murmured. "No . . . ," Mike said, vague and looking away, "I should go." He looked back at me. "Why don't you come up with me?" I looked down with a half smile and shook my head. "I don't want to leave Charlie," I said.

Mike's four dogs—Cupcake, a blue heeler; John, a border collie; Pita, a mountain cur hound; and Jake, a retired hound–border collie cross—knew coyotes and didn't fear them; they worked alongside Mike and lured coyotes in for Mike to shoot. Pita, though sweet toward people, was especially vicious—when they found a den, Pita dove in and killed the pups with a snap of her jaws. Mike and I were both nervous to have Charlie at his house for fear the dogs would hurt him. And so after one long, lingering kiss, Mike went to his house alone and I stayed at the cabin with Charlie.

After losing my job as a substitute teacher, I threw myself into writing, on faith alone, the story of my Vespa journey across the country. I also started leaving Charlie outside for periods of time while I worked in the cabin; he loved it and needed it but I simply couldn't be outside with him watching him all day long—it made me a nervous wreck. I bought Charlie a tiny, thin collar with silver studs on it, so small I could have worn it as a bracelet, which Charlie accepted easily and immediately. I hoped that if Charlie was seen, the collar might deter someone from shooting him, and I wanted him to get used to both collar and leash while he was young. Though we didn't need a leash on our walks, I used one every few days to get Charlie accustomed to it while I could easily control him. I rarely tied him up outside as he was good about staying in the draw below the cabin near the little tamarisk tree; even so, I checked on him so often it bordered on neurotic. Once, I stepped away from the computer to watch Charlie from the top of the draw as Mike's horses happened to wander into the meadow from over the hill. As the horses approached him, still a hundred yards away, Charlie dashed up the draw, past me, and straight to the cabin door. Witnessing this eased my anxiety a bit, proof that Charlie knew the cabin was home and safety, but I still worried while he was out alone and usually ended up taking my laptop and sitting in the grass with Charlie, writing to the hum of bees in the tamarisk boughs.

Generally, Charlie was so affectionate I had to remind myself he was born wild, that he was a coyote, though he fully gave over to his wild nature when he was scared. While out on a walk together, Charlie stepped on one of the flat, round cacti, that speckled the hillsides. He yelped in surprise and held his paw to his chest, but wouldn't allow me to remove the spine from his paw. When I reached down to help him, he bared his teeth, as if my advancing toward him was an additional threat, or he felt the need to defend himself. He made a noise almost like a frog, and snapped at my hand with lightening reflexes in an undeniable feral defense. I was quick enough to keep from getting bit,

but resigned, and gave him space as he attempted to extract it with his teeth. After seeing his fear and panic whenever an unfamiliar car went up the driveway, I discovered eye contact was the most successful and immediate way to transmit information to Charlie, both for discipline and for comfort when he was frightened, and he began to look to me for protection when he was scared.

Still, I needed to stay hyperaware of what he was capable of. And also of what people in town were capable of. When word got out about Charlie, I had no idea what to expect. Charlie was on the bridge between wild and domestic, and I didn't know what that would mean for him, what it would mean as he grew toward adulthood. Would he be stranded between two worlds, or would he be able to straddle both, and "ride the rainbow," as my friend Linda put it.

A storm hit in the night with no real warning before the violence was upon us. In Wyoming, the extremes reign—rain does not drizzle, it floods from the sky in a torrential downpour, like a bucket of water being dumped over the land from a great height. The red dirt becomes slick and sticky and deep; two days later it would be dried out again, back to dust. Growing up in Seattle, it rained all the time but I could walk in it all day long and never really get wet; no one owns an umbrella. Here, one rain drop hit me in the ear once and I almost cried.

Along with the rain came wind, insane wind gusting to forty miles an hour, wind that blew with such force that it pushed the rain through the seams between the logs and the cement chinking and my cabin floor flooded from rain coming in through the walls. The cat, the coyote, and I had a slumber party in bed but never slept, as is usually the case with slumber parties, and I lay there in the dark listening to the water dripping off the roundness of the logs, dripping steadily onto my floor. Charlie and Eli were curled up side by side near my chest, Eli betraying his aloof demeanor by gently grooming Charlie as the two drifted to sleep. By morning the rain was over, puddles covered half my floor, and the wind continued. The wind ripped over the cabin like thundering waves, drying out the land, drying out the moisture the night had brought before it had a chance to reach roots. When the wind came in, I got nothing done—I could not read or write or work. When the wind came in, I was proud of myself for staying alive. Even the spiders crept through cracks in the cabin logs to escape and hide in my bed.

That evening, I left Charlie in his box and met friends down at the Saloon. Mike didn't like socializing in town and though I didn't go out very often, I couldn't remember one time he had ever joined me, so I gave up inviting him and went down on my own. The Saloon was warm and humid, noisy with jukebox and chatter. Everyone was telling stories about the wind, as release, as a way to commiserate. Joslyn had parked her three-quarter-ton wood-paneled truck in front of her house and left it in first gear, yet when she glanced out the window, it was gone. The wind had blown her truck down the street, down a hill at the edge of town, and into a pasture, where she found it sitting deep in alfalfa after it had taken out a fence, barely missing a tree and a trailer house on its way. Her sister Annie had gone on a dump run with her fiancé, and after they unlashed the garbage bins from the back of the truck and emptied them, the wind caught the trash cans and whipped them out of their hands and sent them sailing and bouncing over the countryside. "The wind blows here because everywhere else sucks," announced one young, drunk, philosophical cowboy, his hat pushed low over his brow.

I left the Saloon after a couple of hours and drove home in the late twilight. The sun had gone down, the land was darkening, a sliver of bright moon hung delicately in the sky ahead. The readerboard had changed, and a single word glowed in the night. *"Grattitude."* The play on words from the mysterious minister made me smile. I was gradually giving up my social life but I didn't really care. I adored my friends and had great fun with them, but I had spent years in smoky bars, late nights, all that. These days, it was more exciting to turn in early, wake up early, and wander the open land with a coyote by my side.

Four

July

When I was young, I rode a neighbor's horse regularly though I never had a formal lesson. They probably thought the horse and I slowly walked the wooded trails behind their house; in reality, the moment the horse and I were on the trails we were in a dead run, racing through the trees on tiny footpaths. Once, we rounded a bend in the trail and a tree had fallen across the path, chest high to the horse. We were already galloping, nearly upon it by the time we saw the tree in front of us. I had no idea what to do; no idea whether if I pulled back on the reins we could stop in time or if that would just slow the horse enough to cause a collision with the tree; no idea if the horse could jump it, or if I could either. I'd never jumped with a horse before. I said silently, in my mind, *Horse, this is all yours. You decide.* I held on to the saddle horn, kept the reins in my hand; but let go with everything else. The horse sailed over the tree, and from then on, we searched the woodland trails for fallen trees to jump.

Mike had two horses and I rode them sporadically, but they were each difficult in different ways. Sunshine, a fat paint, was sweet and gentle but would only follow another horse. He had a wonderful demeanor and was full of kindness and affection, but the only time I got rides from him were when I would climb on him bareback, and lie on his back, spine to spine, daydreaming and watching the clouds as he wandered the pasture and grazed.

Houdini was a huge bay and a great ride but the moodiest horse I'd ever known. Some days I could hop on him bareback and lope down the shoulder of the county road with Sunshine following behind us on a lead, or sit in the middle of the pasture and have Houdini lie down next to me and rest his giant head in my lap while I rubbed his face. Other days, Houdini did everything in his power to get me off his back by bucking or biting. Once, he raced straight up a draw with me in the saddle and aimed for the low diagonal between a telephone pole and the supporting guy wire in a vicious attempt to decapitate me. While I was off balance, leaning sideways to avoid the guy line, Houdini began bucking madly until I flew off. As I lay in the dirt trying to remember how to move my eyeballs, Houdini walked three feet up the bank from where I lay sprawled, stretched out his body, and took a long, slow, streaming piss. His not-so-subtle statement trickled down the hill and soaked into my pant leg as Sunshine, who had been following us, ambled over to nuzzle my face with his soft nose and make sure I was still breathing. I joked to Mike that his horses had the same personalities we did—grouchy, angry Houdini, who wanted love deep down but refused to show it too often, and happy-go-lucky Sunshine, who was all about peace and freedom.

By the end of June, I decided I was ready for the commitment of another animal in my care, ready for a horse to call my own. I was enjoying my life among the four-leggeds. I was learning that animals kept me accountable in a way that was all too easy to skirt when living alone or interacting only with people. Animals were honest and true, and they demanded, in their firm, gentle way, the same in return. I wanted a horse that was well-broke and well-trained enough that I could trust it and learn from it, but one with enough energy so as to not be a plodder. And I didn't want to spend more than $1,500. No one believed I would find a horse like that for that amount of money, but within a week, an acquaintance in Cody called and said he had talked to a guy who simply had too many horses and needed to sell a few, and that he might have what I was looking for. I drove up to Cody and spent three hours on a beautiful eight-year-old sorrel gelding with a flaxen mane named Ranger, and though he was the first horse I looked at, I knew he was the one I was looking for. I left a check for half his amount as a deposit and Mike and I drove up with a trailer three days later and brought Ranger home.

Ranger lived in the pasture that spread out beside the cabin so I could spot him out my window and while Charlie and I were on walks. He was easy to catch, but after a few rides through the BLM behind Mike's house, Ranger started acting up. He began balking at the gate to the BLM and refused to go through it, then he refused to go up the driveway to Mike's to reach the gate to the BLM. It got to the point where he would balk the moment I got on him, tossing his head violently, refusing to budge. After four days of this behavior, I wondered what I had done to ruin my horse, sucked up my pride, and left Ranger saddled, tied in the shade of a tree, knowing Mike would be in from work in the next hour or two.

When Mike pulled up, I met him in the driveway and asked if he would take a spin on Ranger, to see if he might know what the problem was. Mike hopped on Ranger and they took off in a fast, fluid trot around the pasture. After three wide circles, Mike reined up beside me and hopped off. "He's fine," Mike said. "He's just got your number. He's seeing what he can get away with. He can sense your hesitation, and maybe he'd rather stand around and get fat rather than work. Show him you're the boss. If he balks, kick him in the ribs."

I got on. I got settled in the saddle, then nudged Ranger with my heels. Ranger didn't move his feet, he put his ears back and tossed his head up and against the reins. I took a breath, stayed calm. Kicked him harder. Ranger began to walk, still tossing his head dramatically but moving forward. And something happened in that moment—I realized Ranger didn't hold the desire to hurt me, just to test me. He wasn't going to start bucking like Houdini so often did—if he were going to buck, he would have done it. And in understanding that, I could trust him, and because I could trust him, I could trust myself while on his back. Ranger was just doing what I had hoped he would do—he was keeping me on my toes, keeping me "on," and asking that I bring confidence and self-control to the relationship so we could work together. I circled Mike once and turned Ranger out for a second test lap. Halfway back, Mike waved across the pasture. I waved back, and Mike walked to his truck and drove up to his house.

When I went out on rides, I tied Charlie in the draw below the cabin. There was one tree halfway between Mike's house and the cabin, and the ground around it was hidden from view of the road by a small hill and the shaping of the landscape. There, Charlie had grass to play in and shade from the shadow of the trunk, and I scattered some of his toys and bones around the tree for him to play with. But though Charlie was sheltered from the road, I worried constantly about his safety while I was out with Ranger. Eagles abounded in the skies above and Charlie was small, defenseless, easy prey. Eagles were no threat to grown coyotes but they were known to take full-grown foxes; Mike had seen an eagle fight a fox and ultimately win, and had witnessed an eagle dive-bomb a young deer over and over until the deer finally collapsed and the eagle tore out its throat. Charlie was smaller than a fox, and he still had the innocence of a young animal. Though I knew Charlie would instinctively bite and fight, he did not have the ability of a mature fox and he had no escape, tied to a tree. Eagles had always been an inspiring treat to catch in the skies along the West Coast when I lived there, but now they were predators. I scanned the sky obsessively, eyes peeled for their dark shapes skimming the air currents. My paranoia, combined with my desire to keep Charlie safe, overtook my reason, and the existence of any eagle sparked intense feelings of vengeful protection. I could be three miles away on horseback, but if I saw an eagle, my heart rate accelerated and became heated, and I was immediately filled with a secret, undeniable urge to shoot it. I was overcome with a visceral desire to destroy anything that might harm Charlie, to kill in order to ensure Charlie's well-being, and I knew I would continue to feel this way until Charlie was large enough to no longer be prey. It should go without saying I now fully understood the way ranchers felt about coyotes. The desire to keep the animals that are in one's care safe from harm, from outside sources, is a powerful one.

By the second week of July, Ranger and I had hit our stride. I came in from a ride and after brushing Ranger and turning him loose in his pasture, I went down to Charlie with the scent of horse still strong on my body. I held Charlie in my lap, as I had been doing after most rides, with the hope that my smell mingling with Ranger's would gradually

assuage Charlie's fear of horses. I refilled his water dish, then walked up to visit Mike while Charlie took a midday nap under his tree.

I found Mike in the basement, sitting at a small workbench, reloading rounds for his 22-250, the rifle he used for his job. I flipped over an empty five-gallon bucket to sit on while he worked. Instead of buying new rounds, Mike picked up the brass casings after he shot and used antique-looking equipment to, as I incorrectly called it, "make new bullets." Bullets were just the tip, one of four parts of a rifle round.

"How's your day going?" I asked.

Mike knocked out the used primer from the base of the tapered brass cylinder with a small hand press and replaced it with a new one; this tiny disk ignited the gunpowder when the trigger was pulled.

"Oh, some of the politics going on in this organization can take the focus away from protecting livestock, meanwhile I'm working overtime to take care of the problem areas where coyotes are getting into sheep."

He measured gunpowder into a tiny brass pan and weighed it on an old-fashioned scale to make sure it was the proper amount, then poured it into the brass casing.

"And I need to put in a fireplace and that's a mess . . ." He trailed off, muttering about time and people and money.

He pressed a .22 caliber bullet into the top and set the finished round in a rack, the last one in a row of others.

"Mike," I said, looking at his hands. They were split and cracked.

"What?" he barked, irritated.

Everything irritated him now. In the eighteen months I had been with Mike, I had noticed what I could only describe as a wave pattern in his life—that he sank deeper into anger and disillusionment whenever things were going well for him and whenever he began to feel happiness. I knew he blamed himself for his daughter's death and believed that if only he had done something different or done something better, she would still be alive. But I believed—had always believed—that connection was still possible between them. I had felt it, and I could see by the extraordinary nature of his eyes that Mike was capable of bridging realms if he chose to. I kept hoping that if I were just funny enough or sweet enough or pretty enough, he would be happy; that I would be more powerful than his fears and his demons—that for me, he would find the strength to live past them. But until he came to forgiveness in himself, for himself, there was nothing I could do; loving him pushed him further away. There was so much about him that felt locked to me.

"Mike, I care, I really do," I said, "but it's the same thing over and over. You don't let yourself enjoy life, because you feel responsible for Tracy losing hers. I don't think you want to be happy, that you say to yourself, 'How dare I enjoy my life when I took hers.' But I will tell you this—Tracy is waiting for you and you're killing her spirit by ignoring her death."

Mike was always self-contained, but after my words he closed himself up completely and looked at me as if he had never seen me before, reptilian eyes looking at me cold, and he stood up and walked out the basement door and drove off with his dogs barking behind him.

I started a new round of irrigating. The pipes in the upper pasture had been sitting for twenty days, and the cows were in that pasture now. The presence of cows made the whole experience of irrigatin' much less peaceful. I never wanted to find myself between a cow and her calf for fear of getting charged and mashed into the ground, and, as I connected the pipes, the cows considered the dribbling sprinklers their own personal drinking fountain. I was constantly chasing them away from the pipe to keep them from knocking the line apart before I had it all joined together.

Rabbits liked to crawl in the ends of the open pipes and hide in them while the water was off, and so when I connected them, I had to make sure I didn't trap a rabbit, for it would plug the whole line and drown when I turned the water fully on. After two irritating hours of battling cows and uncooperative pipe in the heat that had reached ninety degrees by eight a.m., I finished, and couldn't wait to get out of the fields; I had spent enough time cursing both cows and line, stepping in mucky cow pies, slapping mosquitoes, and giving the finger to all animate and inanimate objects around me.

After checking in on Charlie, I went up to Mike's to do dishes, knowing he was out. While there, I washed my face and dried it on the towel hanging in the bathroom and was overwhelmed by the smell of him and the tears began. How was it that I could dry my face on his towel for days and weeks and months but it was only now, three days since we had last spoken, that I registered his smell? I impatiently waited for the dishwasher to finish its course; I waited outside, felt uncomfortable in his house.

Why does being miserable so often drive us into discovering something wonderful? The heat was unbearable in the valley, and when I returned with my dishes, I knew I couldn't stand being in the cabin. Even Charlie was panting, sprawled on the sheet that now covered the bed. We were in and out so much; muddy paws and red dirt made it impossible to keep anything clean. I was resigned to the red mud we all tracked around and the clay dust that seemed everywhere, that settled in a layer on the surface of my coffee when I set the mug on the counter for even a moment, and I draped sheets I got at a thrift store over my bedspread. The cotton sheets were cool and soft to lie against and I didn't care how stained they got with rust-colored streaks from Charlie's feet.

I was hot, tired; my muscles were tense deep inside from things falling apart with Mike. I had to get out of the setting that had become my daily life, had to leave and find something new and solid and beautiful. And so I clipped Charlie to his rope, led him out to my truck, and when I opened the door he hopped up on the running board and into the truck. Charlie and I had spent time in my truck with it parked and then idling in the driveway, and now, after several such sessions, I figured it was time for us to go for a ride. I opened the wing windows halfway for each of us and headed toward the mountain, both for the drive and the hope of cool air. Charlie went from window to window once we started moving, clambering over my lap, sitting with his paws on the windowsills, his ears slightly sideways, then pivoting forward as curiosity trumped his apprehension. He settled into the passenger seat as I took my favorite dirt road up the side of the mountain. The rise was gradual and the red dirt gently gave way to gray and sand-colored rock; dirt draws disappeared, replaced by rocky canyons speckled with craggy junipers. I pulled over and parked on the shoulder and Charlie and I jumped out and walked away from the road. We found an abandoned stock tank running with cool water and I dipped my arms in up to the shoulder, then stood in the tank to cool my legs and cupped handfuls of water to let it run over my belly while Charlie played coyly with the overflow. The water on my skin cooled me and dried instantly. Charlie and I walked further, across a gentle sage meadow to the edge of a canyon layered with a natural terrace of flat stone. I stretched out on the warm stone with my back against a boulder, surveying the swells and drops of the landscape around me as a cool breeze whispered across my face and Charlie explored everything within reach of his rope.

Dark storm clouds covered the sky to the west, a heavenly sight, a reason to hope for rain to reach the valley and wash the dust out of the air. The only sound was the slight wind pushing the clouds and rustling the junipers. It was as if humans didn't exist; and that, to me, in that moment, was paradise. The land was always there; it never deserted, never failed to elevate any mood of mine, just by looking out at a tree or a hillside, the ocean, the mountains, the moon, to the border between clouds and sky.

Charlie ran toward me, up onto my chest with the gift of a lick, joy and happiness radiating from his lean body. The soft downy dome of his head was the last trace of baby about him. Over the course of three months, his eyes had turned from baby blue to a bright turquoise-teal, then to green, then olive, and now they were yellow coyote eyes. I couldn't help but breathe lighter, freer, when he looked up at me with his grin of happiness; it was as if Charlie sensed my frustration and sadness and said, with his golden eyes, *There's no time for that here* . . . And in that space, there was no possession, no ownership, no need for control, nothing beyond the moment of enjoying what we had.

The following day was hot as well. I considered going up the mountain again but at $20 per trip in gas, I couldn't manage it, so the animals and I stayed home and hung around the cabin. Mike and I had found two gigantic, round, aluminum stock troughs at the dump—they were a bit dented in places but otherwise in excellent condition, and we had gone back with a trailer and brought them home. One was ten feet in diameter, and Mike left it on the hill behind his house until he decided where and how to use it. The other one was about six feet across, and Mike and I put it beside the cabin and plugged a few leaks with bark and wood. Filled with water, it became my rustic wading pool. It was the perfect size to sit fully inside, with water up to my shoulders and my legs stretched out across the bottom. The water, heated only by the ambient temperature, never got warm, but it wasn't cold; it was perfectly refreshing for a soak on hot days until I felt just a tiny bit chilled, at which point I would get out and lie on the dusty boards of the deck until I got so hot I had to get in the tub again. Eli stretched out in a deep spot of shade at the base of one of the three trees that stood beside

the cabin, and Charlie was content to sprawl half in the tall grass, half in the mud, chewing determinedly on a thick slice of watermelon and snapping flies out of the air.

Mike barreled down the driveway past the cabin. He didn't wave, didn't honk in acknowledgment like he often did. Maybe it was the space he needed to collect his feelings in order to have a conversation instead of a yelling match, but it always felt like punishment to me. I couldn't live with grudges and half-finished arguments, the games of many relationships. I wanted everything out in the open, immediately. I clipped Charlie to his rope and tied it to the cabin, confident he was hidden from view in the tall grass behind the trees, threw one of Mike's old ripped-up shirts over my bikini, jumped in my truck and took off after him. Mike pulled over in the church parking lot when he saw me in his rearview mirror, riding his bumper. The readerboard had been changed. *"Life—The Whole Loaf,"* it now read. The minister was getting obscure.

We parked window to window. "Mike, you're pushing me away with everthing you've got," I blurted out. "Look at me and tell me that's what you want and it'll be over, or else end this grudge. I can't play games, I can't be in limbo like this."

Like some kind of karmic rubberband, the farther we seemed to pull apart, the stronger it always snapped us back together.

Mike tilted his head slightly and huffed out a laugh. "I know you're not the only one who's thought every bit of what you said. You're just the only one bold enough to say it."

We stared at each other, then smiled at each other, the smile of forgiveness, and, at the base of it, of friendship and respect, of the understanding that we never wanted to hurt each other, even though we often seemed to hurt each other the most. And then we opened the doors of our trucks and got out to embrace. When I stepped out in his tattered shirt with my bikini showing through it and bare feet on the pavement, Mike raised his eyebrows in mock lust but his eyes softened, like what he really saw in it was that I would dash off barefoot and half dressed just to get things out and clear between us. "I'm sorry," he said, and though it was not our first argument, it was the first time he had said he was sorry.

My uncle once said to me, "Love is tolerance," and at the time, I thought the statement was so incredibly cynical and unromantic. But standing there on tiptoes on the hot pavement, looking at Mike and seeing so much hope and sadness in his eyes, I understood it, and he is right. And it hit me, how so much of my behavior toward Mike—though spurred by love—had actually been an attempt to control. I couldn't make his decisions for him. I loved him, and therefore I had to trust him, had to believe in him, had to allow him his own time and support him, or else not be with him.

Charlie was eating more and more. Every day, I put a package of frozen elk on the cabin roof to thaw. I fed Charlie meat twice a day but did not leave his bowl out for him to eat at will, for once he ate his fill, he took the remaining meat and hid it all over the cabin—in every corner, behind my printer, even in bed under the covers. Along with meat and dog food and cat food—Charlie ate whatever he saw Eli eat and therefore snacked on cat food—I gave Charlie raw eggs from Mike's chickens and tastes of nearly everything I ate. He loved cheese as much as I did, and would climb up my chest to eat ice cream out of my mouth if I did not give him a dish of his own.

One afternoon, I was desperate to get some work done but Charlie wanted to play, so I rolled a grape onto the floor in hopes he would entertain himself with it. He chased after the grape and pounced on it, took it in his mouth and tossed it in the air above his head, chased after it, and batted it across the cabin floor. He was engrossed in a full gymnastic floor routine with the grape, and instead of working, I sat at my desk watching him, laughing out loud at his antics. After twenty minutes of play, Charlie dropped to his haunches and slid down to his belly with the grape between his paws and ate it up. I then gave him a stem of grapes and Charlie pulled the grapes off of the stem one by one, and flung them around the room with a toss of his head.

The next day, I noticed Charlie was suddenly interested in a half-charred pine log, blackened and long forgotten after I had thrown it in the snow during some woodstove disaster the previous winter. When we went outside, Charlie went straight for the log and started eating the charred wood. After four days of this strange behavior, I received an email from Jenny, my best friend from third grade, who lived in Boston with her husband. Though we rarely saw each other, we were still close, and she received my photos every day. When she saw a photo of Charlie in the midst of a grape orgy, she wrote to alert me that grapes were poisonous to dogs. I immediately cut off Charlie's grape supply and emailed Jenny about Charlie's bizarre charcoal-eating behavior. She was amazed; charcoal had been the remedy the vet gave Jenny's Persian cat after she ate deadly lily stamens out of the floral arrangement on Jenny's dining room table. I was never positive that Charlie was self-medicating, but I never saw him gnawing on the blackened log once I stopped sharing grapes with him.

At three months, Charlie had not yet caught or killed anything aside from the bugs he pounced upon in the tall grass. He did not actively chase the rabbits we saw on our walks, though he did study them with interest, as he did the three white geese that had taken up residence near the cabin. The geese normally lived down at the corrals among the cows, but when the cows left for mountain pasture, the geese moved over to my cabin. They liked the shade trees and the mud from the horse trough overflow, and made it their new home base. They wandered the perimeter of the horse pasture on daily walkabouts, always the three of them together, and slept under the trees beside the cabin.

They were large geese and had intimidating knobs on the tops of their beaks, and whenever I had been down at the corrals, they had hissed at me with necks outstretched and their pointy tongues sticking out. If I turned my back, I could hear their feet slapping against the dirt as they ran up behind me until I whirled around, whereupon they would stop in their tracks and give me very cocky looks like, *We weren't trying to attack you, you're sooo paranoid.* It got to the point where I always walked away from them backwards and carried pebbles to defend myself.

When Charlie moved in, the geese changed their attitude toward me. After seeing me with Charlie, they either thought I had become a potential predator because I hung out with a coyote, or they knew I was keeping them safe from Charlie—who I kept on a leash when the geese were in the immediate vicinity—and were grateful. The geese and I peacefully coexisted, though Charlie watched them intently, with lust in his eyes, and I could lure him anywhere with a goose feather.

Charlie and I woke with the sun, and in midsummer that meant four a.m. At that hour, the cabin was cool from the window left open all night, and the quiet mornings were soft and pastel for a few delectable hours before the harshness of midday heat arrived. Charlie licked my face sweetly, his eyes gazing into mine, his body soft against my bare shoulder. Charlie loved mornings as much as I did. "Sweet pea," I sang to him, "Sweetest of peas." I spotted the geese from the window; they were at the far end of the pasture, and so I opened the cabin door for

Charlie to investigate what might have changed in the night while I pulled on jeans and a tank.

By late July, Charlie and I were venturing far and wide, exploring much more of Mike's forty acres. We traversed the hills that separated the cabin and the corrals to the south, all the way down to the BLM fence at the eastern edge of the property. Eli usually joined us on our morning walks, and if Charlie and I left the cabin before Eli had returned from his night escapades, he met up with us down in the meadow or traipsing through the sage, somehow finding us no matter where we happened to be. Eli's appearance on these walks brought me a secret smile, for the indifference he so often projected was betrayed by the simple demonstration of finding us afield.

Charlie and Eli were deep into their brotherhood. On every walk, they stopped under a bushy weed and crouched together, eating the tender grass that grew green beneath it. We passed the large tree where I left Charlie during my rides, and Eli dashed up the trunk and into the highest branches, and upon reaching the top, turned and scrambled straight down again. Eli climbed the tree every day we passed it, just for the fun of it, and it didn't go unnoticed by Charlie. As the cat's lanky body streaked past him on his way back down, Charlie reached his front legs up onto the trunk, and stood there, facing the tree on his hind legs with an expression that illustrated his puzzlement: *OK, I reach my front legs up, then what?*

Charlie still followed me without a leash, and though he wandered off to sniff at things, he looked around for me and raced back over. Recently he had gotten so fast, he could outrun me if he chose to and I wondered if independence would trump his childlike obedience. Weeds grew tall in the wide, flat lowland, and when Charlie was focused in one direction, sniffing or pawing at the ground, I lay down and let the grass hide me. I kept a small part of myself visible in his range of view, like

an elbow or a foot, and made little noises, peering through the grass to watch him find me. After a few exchanges like this, I had him find me on sound and scent alone.

Charlie, Eli, and I returned from our walk just as Mike was driving down from his house. He stopped at the cabin. He was building a rock wall around the front of his house and was dusty, sweaty, dirty. "Mind if I dip in your tub?" he asked.

"Not at all," I said.

"You coming in, too?" he asked, as he kicked off his shoes and stripped off his jeans so that he was naked. He held out his hand, and I joined him.

Five

I woke up with the smell of smoke on the air. I pulled a sundress over my head and went out to water my strawberry plant which grew in a plastic hanging pot, out of reach of Charlie and any local rabbits. The moon hung translucent in the pinky-blue prelude of sunrise, the sun not yet up but glowing behind the mountain. I saw smoke to the east, like a blue film, like a ghost; I had no idea where it was coming from or why. Most likely a fire on the mountain.

Charlie poked his snout out the crack of the partially open door. I knelt and opened it so that Charlie walked into me, and with an arm around his body, I clipped him to the long rope I had tied in front of the cabin. Charlie was at the stage where half the time he looked young and small, and the other half he looked like a real coyote. His tail had gone from rat-like to fluffy and was beginning to fill out; his legs, so thin and spindly, were disproportionately long and ended in platter-sized paws. Tufts of fur grew out at his cheeks in thick points and, together with his nose and ears, made his face the shape of an upside-down star. One afternoon, Charlie had been sleeping on the bed in a deep, deep sleep, and when he woke I swore he was an inch taller and an inch wider. He was twice the size of Eli, big enough and quick enough that I kept him on a long line while he was outside. I let Charlie off-leash to run uninhibited when we were on walks, but he could no longer wander freely all the time. Though I felt confident that he would return to the cabin, I knew if someone happened to spot Charlie trotting through the pasture or along the county road without me at his side, he would be shot. It was simply the way things were.

Eli ambled up the driveway in his deliberate way, returning from his nighttime escapades. "Kitten!" I called out in welcoming. Charlie ran toward the cat with his head and shoulders dragging along the ground so as to be lower than Eli, his tail wagging so frantically he nearly shook himself in two, eager to cover Eli's reluctant face in kisses. Eli kept walking his line, sending Charlie in a hop to the side. Charlie circled and caught up to Eli again and Eli softened, ever so slightly, and leaned his body into Charlie's, wrapping his tail over Charlie's back.

It was another day I'd woken not feeling right—my energy was on a steady decline and I felt "halfway" all the time, like the feeling of waking up too abruptly from a nap. It felt like my body existed but only as a shell, and there was nothing inside, nothing behind the skin. I tried to push it aside; my priority was making sure Charlie had enough exercise, freedom, and stimulation. It was what he deserved, and it was my responsibility and my great concern.

I let Eli in the cabin, pulled on boots, untied Charlie's rope, and together we left in the shy light of morning to trot down the familiar beaten trail down the draw below the cabin. At the tamarisk tree, I unclipped Charlie from the rope. He ran in a great circle, sniffing the familiar area, then took off running out into the meadow, sleek and fast. Like a boomerang, he spun around halfway across the meadow and, without losing any speed in the turn, ran straight toward me, a huge grin spread wide across his face, his ears pinned back on his head. Our eyes locked. I crouched low on the ground, grinning myself. Charlie shot past me like a torpedo, just inches from my side, as close as he could get without grazing me, and ground to a halt behind me. He turned, nipped me playfully on my hand, and raced back out. I sank into the grass; just the short walk down the draw had drained my energy. Charlie hit the invisible boundary we had established and turned to race back to me. His yellow eyes gazed deep into mine. I returned the look, and it seemed something registered deep within both of us.

I tied one end of Charlie's rope through the eye socket of a fox skull I found under the tamarisk tree, left there after one of our walks. Charlie ran up into my lap to see what I was doing. I nudged him off and tossed the skull into the meadow while holding the other end of the long rope. Charlie raced over to the skull, and right before he reached it he hurled himself into the air and somersaulted onto it, full of bliss, then grabbed the little skull and shook it. When he dropped it, I slowly drew in the rope and the little skull bounced along the ground as I dragged it back to me. Charlie ran along beside it, his nose to the ground, never taking his eyes off the skull. I tossed it again and we repeated the scene. Soon, Charlie brought the skull back to me after each throw, and I no longer needed the rope. He had figured out the game.

After several returns of the skull, Charlie stood facing me, his face framed by the purple, feather-like blooms of the tamarisk tree. A streak of bright red blood in his mouth stood out against the dusty, muted tones of the land. I pulled Charlie in close and with him on my lap, I opened his jaws and saw a tiny jagged back tooth dangling sideways, blood welling up at his gum. He was losing his baby teeth! I ran my finger around his mouth and felt the giant nubs of adult teeth pressing just below the gum line, and saw where he had already lost a tooth. Charlie had several loose teeth which I left for nature to drop, but his back tooth was flopping against his jaw, barely attached, and I plucked it out and tucked it into the coin pocket of my jeans.

As Charlie grew older, it was striking to witness how delicate he was, not just in body, but in his manner. He took meat from my fingers with the very tips of his teeth, never groping it out of my hands or snapping for it as Mike's dogs did; and licked my face with soft, deliberate little licks. Though Charlie was joyously playful and gangly and eager, his movements and mannerisms were refined, almost aristocratic; quite opposite the familiar image of wild beasts as slobbering and barbaric. I had noticed there was something so similar between Charlie and the deer that regularly passed by the cabin, but for the longest time, I couldn't put my finger on what it was. It wasn't just their coloring, or their oversized ears, or their long, spindly legs. And then I realized it was their posture. These wild animals hold such alertness, and such an incredible elegance, in their posture; something people seem to have lost.

Back at the cabin, I clipped Charlie's rope to the cable runner that Mike and I had stretched along the pasture, up to a group of trees against the hill that separated Mike's house from my cabin. Here, Charlie had a wide area to explore and dig up prairie dogs, and still had access to the cabin door if he wanted to come in. From certain angles and vantages, Charlie was visible from the road while he was on the runner and I only let him out there while I was home. I no longer listened to music if he was out. Instead, I trained my ears on every outside sound, and was ready at any moment to dash out if I heard a car even slow down. But for now, I collapsed on the bed, devoid of energy, and stared at the patterns and faces in the grain of the logs.

Mike was finally putting in a fireplace, something he had looked forward to for years. He cut a giant hole in the side of his log house with his chainsaw and worked alongside a crew of stoneworkers as they poured concrete, wired the firebox, and built a chimney up the side of his house. For two weeks, the crew drove past the cabin in the early mornings on their way to Mike's. Charlie knew Mike's truck by sight and sound and was comfortable riding in mine, but his natural reaction to all other vehicles was to zigzag frantically at the end of his line in an attempt to run away and hide down at his little tamarisk tree, which meant he ran across the driveway. The first morning of work at Mike's house, I heard the even clanks of the crew's truck crossing the cattle guard and dashed out to crouch next to Charlie, who was already outside, in the dirt beside the cabin. I held him tightly against me both to comfort him and to keep him from running across the driveway. I nodded in acknowledgment as the crew drove ever-so-slowly past, staring in disbelief at the coyote I hugged to my body. And with that, the secret of Charlie's existence was out. The four stoneworkers knew about him, and in a town of three hundred, that was significant.

Mike assured me they were great guys and that they proved to be. I didn't worry that they would do anything to Charlie. But I knew how word spread, and that what some might call gossip was considered by others a pastime, a hobby, and definitely entertainment. When I had first moved to Ten Sleep, I learned that nothing happens without someone seeing it or overhearing it and telling someone else. Secrets seemed futile. Living among people who had such open knowledge of

each other's lives could drive a person crazy, or it could be accepted and looked at like a large family. I discovered that the more you know others know about you, the harder it is to judge them. Regardless, soon the town would know about Charlie and that made me nervous. I had been discreet about raising a coyote out of respect for the status quo, and though I knew word of Charlie was bound to come out, I wished I could hide him forever.

The summer heat continued to intensify, and by the end of the first week of August, it hit 110 degrees. Charlie and I tried to endure in the cabin for as long as we could, but by one-thirty in the afternoon we were both miserably sprawled on the bed. Charlie was stretched out long and thin, his head flat against the sheet, panting heavily, while I felt on the verge of a heat-induced coma and knew if I remained there much longer I would lose all strength and will to move. I groggily pushed myself into a sitting position, searched the floor with my toes for flip-flops and slid them on. I clipped Charlie to his leash and scooped him up and carried him to my truck. He hopped over the center console into the passenger seat and I crawled in after him, and drove us up to Mike's and the promise of air-conditioning. It was too hot to even think about walking.

The workmen were outside, high on a scaffolding laying cinder blocks up the side of Mike's house. I parked below the house by the basement door so that Charlie and I could slip directly into the basement without Charlie having to confront the sight of strange trucks and people. Charlie was nervous to go in the basement door—it was new to him, he had never seen it before. With the help of the leash and much cooing, I coaxed Charlie inside and let him off his leash so he could sniff around and explore the unfinished basement, which he went into wholeheartedly. The basement had a cement floor and exposed framing. Mike's tools sat at one end and storage boxes at the other; dirt and sawdust coated the floor. A queen-size log bed was set up in the center of the room, left from when Mike's relatives had visited almost a year before. Charlie and I settled on the bed. I had brought my writing with me and Charlie was content to nap, and we made ourselves comfortable in the quiet and deliciously cool basement, away from the activity and presence of others.

After an hour, I went upstairs to get water for us both, leaving Charlie safe in the basement. The work crew happened to be outside and Mike was at his desk doing paperwork, wearing dusty jeans, shirtless, his reading glasses at the end of his nose. The wall along the log staircase caught my eye. What had been empty space now showcased a gorgeous handmade cradleboard, a Native American-style baby carrier, made from the softest deer suede and mounted on stained wooden slats that formed a frame so it could be worn like a backpack or set securely against a tree. It was intricately beaded and decorated with leather fringe tipped with beads and the tiny dew claws of mule deer that gently clacked together as I ran my fingertips through the fringe. Mike looked up as if nothing were out of the ordinary, but in answer to my raised eyebrows, he said dismissively, "I dug out Tracy's cradleboard from the basement. Hung it up finally."

"It's incredible," I murmured, and got water and a dish for Charlie, and returned downstairs.

The crew pulled out at five, gravel crunching under their tires as they rolled past the basement windows. I opened the door leading upstairs and Charlie bounded up, looking in every direction at once for Mike, and ran over to him with ears folded back and tail wagging. He curled onto one shoulder and rolled over on his back, and Mike grinned and reached down to rub Charlie's belly. Charlie always peed a little under Mike's hand, out of excitement or submission or a combination of the two. I perched on one of the counter stools. Mike was eating toast with jam on it and pulled off a piece, about to give it to Charlie.

"No, wait!" I said. "He has to sit before he gets food now."

Mike looked at me like I was crazy. "Really," he said, almost as a challenge.

"Yeah," I said. "Here, give it to me." I held out the strawberry toast to Charlie.

"Sit, Charlie," I said.

Charlie sat.

"Good job, baby!" I praised, as Mike nearly fell off his chair.

"I can't believe you taught a dang coyote to sit." Mike was truly dumbfounded.

"It's as much Charlie as it is me," I said. "He's just so good! He's such a happy being and wants everyone else to be happy too."

"Unbelievable."

Charlie licked all the jam off the bread and then turned to explore a flower pot, leaving the toast on the floor behind him.

"See," I said to Mike, "He's a gluten-free coyote, too!"

I was feeling worse daily, overtaken with lethargy, and I had developed a strange pointed cough that would not go away. When my body didn't function at its peak I felt pathetic. I believed my body would eventually fight off whatever was going on inside; it would have to. My health insurance had an extremely high deductible and I didn't have enough money to go to a doctor. I still photographed Charlie nearly every day–I was simply compelled to, and Charlie was a natural in front of the camera, with an ability to look down the lens straight at the viewer–and still sent out a photo a day via email to my friends and family. In the second week of August, I got a call from Jenny, my childhood friend. "I just cannot

tell you how much I love getting your photos every day!" she said. "And I forward them on to my friends and my family and now they can't live without them either. And I was thinking, you really should be getting paid for this. I mean, I know it must take time for you to do it, and for all of us in the city, it's just the most wonderful thing to get every day."

I had never considered opening up the "Daily Coyote" emails to the public, and for profit, but after a brief debate, and because I was so broke I was buying gas $6 at a time, I set up a very basic website with a handful of photos chronicling Charlie's growth, and a sign-up field that allowed anyone to receive the daily photos for five dollars a month.

By mid-August, Charlie was big enough to introduce to Mike's dogs. With Charlie on his leash, we walked up to Mike's and found Cupcake, John, and Pita sprawled in the grass and under the deck. Charlie was thrilled to be in their presence, eager to be friendly and play. He dropped down onto his elbows in front of Cupcake, but she growled at him, and snapped at him whenever he got too close. She did not want to know him. Charlie turned tight circles beside her a few times but her reaction to him never changed, so he wandered off toward John. With tail wagging, he dropped down into the play-stance in front of John, but John turned and scuttled away. He seemed afraid of Charlie, and trotted off quickly when Charlie tried to follow him. Charlie turned to Pita, who was stretched out in the shade of the deck. He pranced up to her and tentatively reached out to sniff her foot. She rolled herself upright and reached her dark nose out from under the deck to sniff Charlie's face, then slunk out and hopped to her feet in the sunlight, her tail wagging in unison with Charlie's, and after circling and sniffing, they began to chase each other around the yard, dropping to their elbows and leaping to play.

Charlie adored playing with Pita, and though he tried to win the friendship of John and Cupcake as well, it never happened. Despite hopes of being their playmate, if Charlie saw Cupcake or John approach me, he stood in front of me with his hackles raised from the crown of his head all the way down his back to his tail in a two-inch Mohawk and growled at them. It was an oddly gratifying feeling, to sit in the grass with Charlie standing in front of me, a stunning display of hackles and fangs. But after a few days, Charlie got used to the group of us spending time together, and he no longer challenged the other dogs when they came near me, happy to accept a place at the very bottom of the totem pole.

One evening, I brought Charlie in when I was ready to go to bed and noticed that clouds had been building, obscuring the stars, preparing for a thunderstorm. Inside, Charlie set off on an absolutely berserk routine like a rambunctious child before bed, jumping on the bed, then off, racing around the tiny cabin room, pulling toys from his toy bowl that sat on the cabinet at the foot of the bed. I got in bed and turned off the light and lay still, a hint that he needed to do the same. His nails clicked across the steamer trunk in the dark on his way onto the bed and he climbed over me and lay down at my knees. I lay there in the dark afraid even to move my feet for fear of setting him off again. When we were finally resting peacefully, about to sink into sleep for the night, Eli jumped into the window box and sat there pressed against the window, meowing plaintively to come in from the rain that had begun. Charlie bounded off the bed, and even in the dark, I knew his tail was wagging. I rolled my eyes and turned on the light. I unlatched the door and opened it a few inches for Eli. Eli hated getting his paws wet, and when I didn't hear him jump down off the window box, I opened the door a bit more to peer around it and see what he was doing. Eli sat crouched in the window box staring at the door; he obviously wanted to come in but refused to jump down to the wet boards of the deck in order to do so. "Eli, come *on*," I ordered, but he just sat there looking at me. In hopes of luring him in, I reached my body just a bit farther out to tap the boards with one pointed toe, and as fat drops splashed against my bare leg and shoulder, Charlie squeezed between the door and my body and out into the dark night. *NO!* I screamed in my mind, somehow seeing everything happen before it did. *The goose, the draw* . . . I dashed to the phone and dialed Mike. Mike was asleep, and he answered just as the desperate honking began outside. "Charlie got out, Mike, he's out without a leash and he's killing a goose!" Mike could hear the goose screaming through the phone. "I'll be right down," he said. I threw on a windbreaker and boots, grabbed a flashlight and went out into the night. There was Charlie, eyes crazed in delight, with his jaws clamped around the neck of a goose nearly twice his size. Lightning bounced off the goose's flapping wings as Charlie trotted through the mud sideways, dragging the goose across the driveway, down the trail to his tamarisk tree.

I saw Mike's headlights bending around the curve of the hill and waited there as he parked. "He's down in the draw," I said, already drenched. "He's got the goose." Mike set off and I followed in the slick mud, and arrived in time to see Mike grab Charlie by the scruff of his neck, flashes of lightning glinting off Charlie's teeth as he snapped in protest, the goose left in the mud as Mike carried Charlie up the draw, swearing loudly and clamping Charlie's jaws together with his hand. I continued down the draw to where the goose lay. I squatted in the grass next to it, stroking the goose from its beak, across its head, down its long neck, tears streaming down my face for the goose that had been so evil to me; I was so sad it had to die this way.

I knew Mike wouldn't go back to his house until I returned, so I tore myself away from the goose and walked back to the cabin. Mike had clipped Charlie to his leash which I had left tied to the front of the cabin, and in the light of his headlights, I saw Mike was bleeding where

Charlie had bit his forearm. Water dripped from his hair and down his neck; he was tired and tense and upset about the goose. He said his arm was probably fine but he wanted to go home to clean it properly, and we said a distracted goodnight.

I went inside and left Charlie outside alone for a few minutes. Once I had collected myself, I went out onto the deck and stood in front of Charlie with a few bits of cheese in my hand. I held one out. "Sit," I said. Charlie sat. I gave him the cheese. Charlie got up and nosed around my leg. I held up another piece of cheese. "Sit." He sat. I was not giving him cheese as a reward for attacking the goose; I did it to focus him, as a rhythmic, methodical balancing of the intense energy that had just been coursing through his system. "Sit." Charlie sat for me. It calmed him visibly.

I took Charlie inside and left him in the cabin with Eli while I went out into the rain again. I had some empty cardboard boxes in the lean-to beside the cabin, and I grabbed one and carried it down the draw to put the goose in, with the intention of letting the goose spend the night in my truck, out of the weather, in hopes it might survive. When I got to the bottom of the draw, the goose was gone. A wide scattering of feathers in the matted grass was all that remained. I swept the area with my flashlight, saw nothing, and returned to the cabin. Eli and Charlie were curled up contentedly, and I stripped off my soaked windbreaker, dried my hair on a towel, and crawled in to bed with them. I lay in the dark, wondering if this event would unlock a part of Charlie that had been latent; if the thrill of the kill would mark a sudden change in his personality, a shift in his behavior.

In the morning, I looked out the window across the pasture and saw all three geese taking their morning walk. Though I could not distinguish between the three from a distance, I saw no sign of limping or trauma from any of them apart from the typical goose-waddle. Charlie, as well, behaved as if nothing dramatic or out of the ordinary had happened. As I waited for the honey to dissolve in my coffee, I called Mike. "The goose survived!" I told him. "You're kiddin' me," he said. I told him of their stroll about the pasture and asked about his arm; he told me it felt fine, and that the bite was not nearly as bad as he had thought.

One aspect of country life I understood conceptually but still had not integrated into habit was planning ahead for the seasons. Planning ahead had never been remotely necessary as a city dweller, and it implied stability and permanence of place. With one winter in the cabin behind me, however, I knew a few amendments would improve my standard of living and level of comfort. I had mentally catalogued the holes and cracks in the cabin from the times the icy wind blew through, making it impossible to stay warm no matter how blazing I got the woodstove. And regardless of wind, a huge amount of heat escaped through the peak of the roof, where my Styrofoam insulation job had left cracks and I could actually see sky if I craned my neck at the right angle.

It was hard for me to work on things for winter when it was nearly 100 degrees, but I knew it was better now than when I was cursing the cold and myself for putting it off. I cleaned out my bureau and used the t-shirts and sweatshirts I no longer wore to stuff between the ridgepole and the peak of the roof. I used aerosol foam to fill the gaps that ran the perimeter of the windows and door, and caulked the north wall of the cabin with silicone chinking to prevent future wind-and-rain storms from flooding my cabin. I had three packages of outdoor rope lights that a friend had given me and I wrapped them decoratively around the support beams and over the doorway of the cabin, so that when it got dark at five, I would have outside light to gather firewood instead of fumbling in the darkness or wearing a headlamp as I had the winter before.

The most important task was stockpiling firewood, as it was my only form of heat. And since Mike now had a fireplace as well, we made several trips up the mountain for wood. It was one of my favorite outings. I loved jumping in the passenger seat of Mike's pickup with nothing but sunglasses and my leather work gloves, loved leaving the town and the valley behind for the rough dirt roads that wrapped their way around the mountain. I loved being on a mission to find the perfect standing dead trees, driving through sagebrush as the tires of the pickup released the heavy scent of sage into the air.

Once we got up the mountain, I wandered aimlessly, taking in the views while Mike felled a tree with his chain saw and cut it into rounds. I carried the rounds to the pickup, the sound of the running chain saw in my ears and the smell of sap and gas and smoke mingling in odd comfort with the surroundings. Sawdust flew around Mike as he steadily cut the tree into lengths he knew made good logs for my woodstove. As Mike felled another tree I made innumerable trips between the fallen tree to the pickup, peering over the logs in my arms to navigate my path through dry grass, sagebrush, and shed branches. After sawing up the second tree, he called out, "Let's take a break; we're in no rush to get back," and we sat together on a log, enjoying the peace we found on the mountain, talking or not talking, letting our breathing slow and our sweat dry. Woodpeckers and squirrels called to one another from the treetops; tiny wildflowers bloomed in their dainty beauty, each no larger than a fingernail, bobbing on graceful, delicate stalks.

"Look at all the wildflowers," I said to Mike, softly. "They're like fairy flowers."

"All I see are all these dead trees," Mike said. "The beetles musta' killed 'em all . . ."

And then he laughed. "Everything you see is for the survival of your spirit, and everything I see for the survival of my body."

When we filled the pickup with logs stacked high as the cab, we slowly made our return to civilization for strawberry milkshakes. Pita and Cupcake rode on the top of the woodpile all the way down, and when we reached the smooth roads in town, Pita moved to the roof of the cab, eliciting stares and quick snapshots from tourists on their way to Yellowstone.

At the end of the month, I went to Worland after putting it off as long as I could; I wasn't fond of doing errands, or leaving Ten Sleep for that matter, and now, when I left, I missed Charlie on top of it and felt guilty for having to leave him tied to his tree while I was gone. I drove past the readerboard then, whose message, *The Courage to Go Fishing,* stuck in my mind, through the heat and barren land of the badlands that separated Ten Sleep and Worland. When I reached town, trees and cultivated lawns lined the streets. The cotton was flying, blowing loose from the cottonwood trees like snowflakes. I glanced at my clock to see how fast I could get through my shopping; after two or three hours in Worland, I always felt like the day had been stolen from me, even when I felt my best. I was still feeling run-down, but better than I had, and my cough was improving. I hit the hardware store, and then, on a whim, crossed the street to the thrift store to look for toys to bring back for Charlie. A bin of stuffed animals sat along one wall and I rummaged through it, passing over the toys that had beans for stuffing, for I knew they'd turn into a mess, and settling on a fist-sized bighorn ram, a floppy-eared bunny, and a large, round, yellow chick, animals he might enjoy in the wild. I spun through the grocery store as quickly as I could, and as I impatiently waited in line to check out, I eavesdropped on the women in front of me. One woman was going into great detail describing how she had been ailing for weeks, and that when she had gone to the doctor, discovered it was West Nile. The symptoms she enumerated were identical to what I had been going through. Apparently, several women in town had gotten West Nile in August, and over a hundred statewide. It was just as well I never went to the doctor; it was a virus, and there was nothing that could have been done anyway.

When I got back to the cabin, I unloaded only the groceries that needed refrigeration, then jogged down to the far tree where I had hidden Charlie. He saw me coming down the path and crouched down, flattened out in the grass, his ears flattened as well, lowered sideways so that they stuck out on each side of his head, parallel to the ground. He kept his eyes on me as I neared, and as I was about to reach him, he leapt forward with his tail wagging and his ears folded back on top of his head, love in his eyes. He fell over onto his side with his paws folded on his chest, trying to reach up to lick my face while wiggling on his back as I knelt beside him and rubbed his belly.

Six

September 7 was the anniversary of Mike's daughter's death. Mike called in the morning to say he was going for a drive in the hills and that he would have his phone turned off, but to leave a message if I needed him, that he didn't want to ignore me but he didn't want to talk to anyone else. Charlie and I went on our morning hike up and down the red dirt draws, this time, venturing across the BLM boundary to explore new territory. Afterward, I left Charlie under the tamarisk tree to watch the late butterflies while I went up to the cabin. But instead of going inside, I sat on the little side deck, staring into the long grass that grew around the wellhead. The year before, Mike and I had been lying on the sofa together wrapped in a blanket, and he had recounted the day of Tracy's death. He and his two daughters were living in town—his wife had left seven years prior, when the girls were three and five—but he had recently purchased the land on which we now lived.

"We spent the day out here," he said. "It was a beautiful day, warm, blue skies. I was working on the cabin, and Kadi and Tracy were running around on four-wheelers—I just let them explore the place while I was sawing up logs for the cabin. There was this moment when everything went silent—I didn't even hear the sound of the chain saw I was using, and I turned it off. Then Kadi came driving up and said—and she said it in the most factual way—'Tracy's flipped the four-wheeler and I think she's dead.' I jumped on Kadi's four-wheeler with her behind me and drove out to where they were . . ."

He began to weep. I lay next to Mike, not saying anything, not prompting him to go on or asking where it had been; I was simply there to listen to however much of the story he decided to tell. It was the first time in the eight years that had passed that he had spoken to anyone about the details of that day.

"When we got there, the four-wheeler was upside down, and I pulled it off her . . ." his face was wet with tears, "and there she was, and her head was smashed and I could see her brains . . ." He trailed off again. "I didn't know what to do—I didn't want to leave her but I took Kadi and drove straight to my brother's house—he lived about a quarter-mile away back then, and they called the ambulance. I left Kadi with them and went back over to Tracy . . . and when the ambulance got there they said she was dead. And then they loaded her up and took her away, and that was the last time I saw her. And I just lay in the cactus and screamed."

It was now the ninth anniversary and I wept, just as I had the day

Mike had told me, and as I blinked away tears for Mike, I suddenly felt the day from Tracy's side as well—the freedom, the joy, the rush; the moving toward something else that we, here, cannot yet explain; the fearlessness, the painlessness. The total sense of immersion was intense; I had to get balanced again. I wiped my eyes on the hem of my shirt and walked slowly down to Charlie who lay in the grass under his tree, peaceful in a nap with a slight smile on his face, lying on his side with his head tilted back, cradled softly in the grass. I knelt at his back and sat there with my legs folded under me and my chin toward my chest, eyes closed, stroking his head and his body and his fur, breathing in with each downward stroke.

I kept petting him, my open hand fitting perfectly across his width. Charlie didn't move but I was gently nudged from my darkness and raised my head to the hill between the cabin and the corrals. Just above the ridge, a cluster of black winged forms swirled in a delicate ballet, circling together gracefully over one particular spot on the hill. I recognized the dark wingspan and tiny heads of vultures. I counted them, twice to make sure of the number. There were fifteen. I had never seen more than three at a time in the skies before. Then, just as gracefully as their circling spirals had been, the vultures glided away, one by one, dissipating into the blue sky until I could not see anything of them.

The scientific name for the turkey vulture, *Cathartes aura*, translates to "golden purifier." According to many cultures, vultures represent a bridge between realms, between the physical world and the world of spirits. In ancient Greece, the vulture was considered the guardian of the mysteries of life and death. The Pueblo Indians believed vultures facilitated contact with the dead, and in Egypt, vultures were linked to the goddess of Truth. I bent down and nuzzled Charlie's neck. He rolled over playfully and I rubbed his belly, starting slow and soft and then with greater and greater friction and he wiggled and squirmed and smiled, then hopped up, ready for fun. I untied his leash from the base of the tree and together we ran up the hillside, up to the crest to where the vultures had been circling just feet above the land. I knew if a carcass was hidden in the sage, Charlie would find it–he could find dried-up newts beneath rocks. We spent forty minutes on the hilltop, and though Charlie sniffed every sagebrush and hopped over cacti, that was all we found.

Back at the cabin, Charlie jumped onto the bed and sank down with a strip of rawhide to chew. Mike had left a message while we were on the hilltop, just a call to say hi, and that he was on his way back in. I was about to call him back when I heard his dogs barking from down the road and his truck cross the cattle guard. Charlie, alert and eager, hopped down from the bed, and together we stood outside as Mike drove toward us.

Mike got out of his truck slowly and went straight for Charlie, who lapped up Mike's attention. After a few rubs and licks, Charlie trotted off in his happy-go-lucky way to try to hang with the big dogs, who mostly ignored him. Mike turned to me with a half smile, a valiant gesture to appear okay, even though he was not.

"How are you?" I asked him once we were in a hug of our own.

"Oh, okay, I guess," he said. "I went for a long walk, called in a coyote . . . I don't know. It's hard."

"Mike," I said, serious but breathless, "you will not believe what happened." I recounted my morning, seeing the vultures, and I pointed to the place above the hill where they had been, and told him of the grace of the sight, the meaning vultures represent, and then the exploration of the hilltop with Charlie, and finding nothing, no physical or logical explanation of why they were there.

Mike stared at me kind of sideways as I told him everything. He took a sigh to brace himself.

"You're not going to believe this," he said quietly, "but that's where they were?"

I nodded.

"That's the very spot she died."

After opening the Daily Coyote photos to the public, word began to spread, slowly but surely, and the subscriptions were bringing in a little money. But I had reached the point where I had to have more income. I was distressed by the fact that Charlie had to be tied up when he was outside, and my dream was to put up a coyote-proof fence, something that would cost at least a thousand dollars. School had been in session since mid-August, and in those three weeks, I had not been called in to sub. My love of teaching inspired me to call a new company in Ten Sleep that taught English to Koreans through one-on-one live internet video sessions. I interviewed with the manager and went through the training process, and found it an ideal job with a flexible schedule. I was amazed by the connection and intimacy that was possible through the video sessions. Korea is sixteen hours ahead of Wyoming, so I taught from five a.m. to eight a.m., which was nine p.m. to midnight in Korea. The students ranged from third-graders to college students to business executives looking to improve their English-speaking skills, but at that hour, I mostly taught college students. I soon had a group of about fifteen "regulars." They were fun and dedicated, and each session was challenging and wonderful for me. With this new schedule, Charlie and I began getting up at four-thirty in the morning. He'd sniff around outside while I got ready, then we'd run down to the far tree between the cabin and Mike's house that was sheltered from view of the road and romp together briefly. Then I'd run back to my truck and drive to the office space in town and teach for three hours. While I loved every second, I looked forward to returning to Charlie. I'd change into grungy clothes and then jog down to meet him. He'd greet me with sparkling eyes and his tail wagging, and we'd take off on our morning hike.

One morning in the middle of September, I woke with Charlie next to me as usual, curled against my side. I flicked on the lamp and before I slid out of bed, Charlie stood on the covers with his back hunched up and started hacking, vomiting a small amount of clear frothy liquid onto the bedspread. "Charlie, baby," I said, and reached up to stroke his back. When I got out of bed, Charlie hopped down the stair steps after me and hung around my legs while I got ready. After a quick cup of tea and a few swipes of mascara, I gathered my papers, clipped Charlie to his leash, and we headed out in the dim light for his tree. About twenty yards down the trail, Charlie stopped and squatted with diarrhea. Combined with the frothy throw-up, it caused me to raise an eyebrow, but we went on our way. I got him settled at the tree, then dashed back up to my car and went to work. Three hours later, I returned and went directly down to Charlie. He was very mellow; happy to see me but less energetic than usual. We walked the path back up to the cabin, and there in the driveway, Charlie had diarrhea again. Back in the cabin, he had no interest in water or food, instead climbing up to the bed and curling up at the foot. I heard dogs barking and looked out the window to see Mike coming down the driveway, heading out late for some reason. I ran out and he slowed down, and I ran around to his window.

"Charlie threw up this morning—like a clear liquid—and then he had diarrhea twice, twice that I've seen, when we were walking down to the tree before work, and then just now."

Mike furrowed his brow. "You don't think . . ." He trailed off. "Did he eat anything out here that was strange? Like if someone threw a piece of tainted meat into the yard?" he asked.

"Uh-uh. Nothing I've seen," I said.

"Well, keep an eye on him . . ."

"What else could it be?" I asked. "Besides poison?"

"Well," said Mike, "it could be Parvo, or distemper, but with distemper there's a bunch of gunk around the eyes, or it might just be that he found something that disagreed with him."

"OK," I said. "I'll keep you posted."

Mike drove off and I went inside. Charlie was curled in a ball. He lifted his eyebrows to look at me. I knew something was terribly wrong.

I got on the internet and read dozens of articles on puppy disease. Symptoms of Parvo included diarrhea and, more uniquely, a clear frothy vomit. Everything I read about Parvo stressed the importance of getting treatment early, how it was imperative to treat the dehydration as soon as possible; puppies that were treated immediately had an 80 percent chance of surviving, whereas puppies that were not treated for a day or more often died. I read like a machine, then reclined on the bed with my body curled around Charlie's. It was Parvo; I knew it was. It was an absolute knowing that I'd had from the moment Mike mentioned the name, that had been corroborated by the documents I read online, and though I was as far from a vet as one could be, I knew it with conviction.

I called Mike on his cell. "Charlie's just lying here, Mike; he hasn't moved. I know something is wrong. I know it's Parvo."

Mike was driving. "Well, just wait and see if he perks up," he said.

"No, Mike. If it is Parvo, it has to be dealt with immediately, like today, like right now. We have to call a vet to see if there's anything we can do. Will you call your vet, or do I need to?" I thought we'd have

a much better chance of getting something, of getting somewhere, if Mike made the phone call, because I had never met the vet; I would be cold-calling about treating a coyote.

"OK," said Mike. "I'll call him here shortly."

"Call him now!" I begged. "Please, Mike."

I knew Mike was not brushing off the seriousness of Charlie's situation. I knew he was uncomfortable with calling the vet, for whom he had shot coyotes off his land, for treatment to save one, and I think he was nervous about exposing himself in that way.

Parvo is an extremely common, easily contracted canine disease. The virus hits the bone marrow so that the immune system is incapacitated. Then it travels to the digestive tract and destroys the intestinal lining. This is where infection can set in, in addition to the virus. Puppies with Parvo have to be given fluids to survive—death is usually caused by dehydration. Most puppies are vaccinated against it. Charlie had not had any vaccinations.

Mike called me back an eternally long half hour later and said he had talked to the vet, and that the vet concurred that it sounded like Parvo. "I'm on my way to the vet's right now," he said. "They're gathering up what we need to treat Charlie and sending it home with me." I thanked him profusely, asked him to hug the vet for me, and asked him to drive home as fast as he could without speeding.

I was lying on the bed beside Charlie, lost in concern and gentleness and softly murmuring to him when Mike knocked on the door. Charlie didn't lift his head as I rose and crossed the cabin to let him in. Mike had a brown grocery bag which he set on the counter. "They told me how to do all this, but you're going to have to do it, you know—I'm too afraid of needles," Mike said, and I giggled for the first time that day as Mike looked at me sheepishly. I pulled out the contents of the bag and laid them on the counter—an IV bag of fluid, complete with a long tube ending in a small needle, and two ziplock bags, each containing three filled syringes. "We gotta get 300cc's of the lactated ringers in him a day, and then one shot is an antibiotic and one is a painkiller. All of them go just under the skin—not in the muscle or veins. If you grab the fur behind his neck, you can get it under the skin there. He said it'll look like Charlie's got half a grapefruit under his skin after you give him the ringers, but it'll absorb into his body." Mike was pale just telling me how to use the needles.

As Mike lay down on the bed between Charlie and the wall, I tapped a nail into the log beam above the bed and hung the IV bag from it. I arranged the two syringes on the mattress and then knelt on Charlie's other side with the IV needle in my hand. I stroked Charlie's head and back, comforting both him and myself while feeling out the area I would be applying the shots. I locked eyes with Mike. He was ready to hold Charlie down when the needle struck. "OK, I'm going to do it," I said, and holding my breath, I pinched the fur above his shoulders and slid the needle in horizontally. I felt the pressure of the needle against his skin, then felt it break through, the tip floating inside his body. I spun the dial on the tube, releasing liquid into the drip. It flowed steadily into Charlie, and Mike and I both held our breath, our eyes darting from the IV bag to Charlie to each other. Slowly, the level of the clear liquid in the bag lowered. Charlie had barely moved, but he began to squirm as the hump of liquid grew under his skin. I held the needle steady in his body and Mike petted Charlie's face to soothe him. "That's a hundred and fifty cc's," said Mike. "That's good for now; we can do another dose later." I spun the dial closed and pulled the needle out as quickly and smoothly as I could, and then let my hands start shaking. Charlie lifted his soft head, his ears cocked to the side, looked from Mike to me, and then lay back down on his paws. I uncapped both syringes, pinched another section of loose skin to the left of the area I had filled with fluid, and with two fast horizontal stabs, depressed their contents. Charlie made no sign of discomfort, and while Mike continued to lie alongside him on the bed, I gathered up the syringes and wound up the IV tube and looped the excess around the nail.

Afterward, all three of us were exhausted. Mike went up to his house while I stayed and rested with Charlie after canceling my teaching sessions for the week. Twice, Charlie delicately hopped off the bed to drink water, but immediately threw up afterward. While he was resting deeply that evening, I decided to try to give him another 150cc's of the ringers, and to try it by myself. Though Mike was always there to help with Charlie, he seemed so stressed by the needles; I didn't want that energy around Charlie if I didn't need it. I unwound the tube from the nail and knelt next to Charlie's sleeping body. I grasped the skin behind his neck and slid the needle in, quickly spun the dial to release the fluid, and sat there petting his body while the fluid collected under his skin. Charlie sighed, but didn't fight it. I slipped the needle out and slipped into bed. Charlie arranged himself in the curve of my waist, and we slept.

I woke up and bent forward over Charlie, petting him; he reached up to lick my chin and then lay back, rolling over to expose his belly for me to rub. We spent a long morning in bed. He got up and drank thirstily, then not a minute later, turned around and threw up, nothing but clear and frothy liquid. He didn't try to eat. Charlie was fairly alert all morning, so Mike came down and together we administered the syringes and the lactated ringers. Charlie fought the shots a bit, which I took as a good sign. We had three days of medicine, and here was Charlie on

day two, showing obvious improvement. Mike was scheduled to teach a hunter safety class and was going to be gone all day, but he said he'd call every chance he got.

Charlie seemed miserable and bored by midafternoon, having done nothing but lie on my bed for nearly two days. He just lay there with his eyes open, looking wistfully toward the door, so, though it made me inexplicably nervous, I took him down the draw to his tamarisk tree. The day was sunny and mild, neither hot nor chilly, and Charlie scratched out a shallow hole and curled up under the tree. He watched the last of the butterflies looping through the air, then tucked his nose under his tail and went to sleep. I thought perhaps the fresh air would help him sleep well that night.

I woke up several times in the night consumed with dread. I turned on the bedside light each time I woke up, and placed my hand on Charlie to both feel and see that he was still breathing. Charlie lay motionless all night, and all morning, too. He slept on the bed, getting up only to drink, after which he immediately threw up. He was weak and wobbly on his legs, and I left the cabin every twenty minutes or so to stand outside and cry. I tried to stay calm and positive around Charlie, but my heart was breaking.

Around noon, I picked up Charlie and carried him out to my truck and we drove to Mike's. The cabin was starting to feel stifling, like a den of sickness, and I thought Charlie might like the change of scenery; he hadn't moved from the bed all day. I parked at the basement door and carried Charlie inside. The bed was still made in the center of the basement, and when I placed Charlie on it, he curled right back up and watched me from under his eyebrows. I got a small Tupperware of water and placed it on the ground near the bed, and then lay on the bed with my body around him, petting him and kissing the incredibly soft fur that still remained between his ears—it had never changed from puppy fur.

I spent the day in the basement, sitting cross-legged on the bed where Charlie slept, obsessively staring at his abdomen to make sure he was still breathing. Charlie was hanging in the balance, and I knew we were each being asked a question–whether we were capable of and willing to stay in this journey together. Charlie had done so much to adapt to life with humans and a stable home. I had tried to do as much as humanly possible to give Charlie what he needed and deserved–freedom and exercise and bits of animal carcasses as well as love. Both Charlie and I had made sacrifices in order to accommodate each other, and we each received gifts that could only have come from being with each other. But I wondered if Charlie was willing to lose so much of his heritage, so much of his wildness; and I needed to figure out if I was truly willing to give up my wildness as well. If either of us was unsure, I knew Parvo would take him. These were difficult questions to ask myself; they required absolute honesty. I bent over Charlie's sleeping form and unbuckled the leather collar from around his neck, so that he could feel free and unhindered, so that he could make whatever choice he needed to make. I rubbed his neck to fluff out the fur. I wanted to stay in it. And I couldn't stop the tears.

In the afternoon, I went outside. Mike was sawing up lengths of logs and stacking them for firewood. Tears streaked my face and the late afternoon sun felt extra bright. "He's gonna be okay, Shreve," Mike said as I cried against his chest. He wrapped me in a hug, then straightened me out and sat me on the tailgate of his pickup. "It's like when I got the plague," he started. Mike was one of a handful of people to survive the bubonic plague, which he had contracted seven years before when he was bit by an infected flea off a coyote he had killed on the job. "I was laid out for weeks fighting it off–I didn't do a thing but lie in bed look- ing gray and on the verge of death. And this is what Charlie's doing. He's lying there fighting it off; this is the best way for him to get better.

He's gonna be okay." And then he hugged me again so I wouldn't see the tears sneaking into his eyes.

Charlie now recognized the needles, and when they came out, his eyes filled with dread, but he did not fight. Mike lay beside him and kept him still and comforted, which allowed me to concentrate on giving the shots properly and holding the IV under Charlie's skin for as long as possible. We now did all the shots and the full dose of the IV at once, to keep the stress minimized.

After we gave Charlie his shots the evening of the third day, I left him downstairs and, emotionally spent, flopped on the sofa upstairs to watch a mindless movie about killer bats with Mike. The movie distracted me for intervals, and then my mind would return to Charlie and I buried my head in the sofa pillows, crying softly and silently. Mike did everything he could to reassure me, to be the solid, stoic shoulder for me, and sometimes it worked and sometimes the woe overtook me completely. When the movie ended, I hugged Mike long and hard, then returned downstairs and slept the night with Charlie in the basement.

It had been four days since Charlie had eaten anything and he still couldn't keep water down. Mike was able to get three more days' worth of medicine from the vet, and we kept our vigil over Charlie. I had sent out a few notes in the Daily Coyote emails about what was going on and was flooded with heartfelt, loving letters from strangers and friends. Many people shared what an inspiration Charlie was for them, how he reminded them of joy and freedom, how he helped them connect with their own wild spirits. That night I sat outside, leaning against the house for a moment alone, the stars close enough to pick like berries. I realized what Charlie had brought me was so very different. I had always been wild; I had always found the joy in little things. Instead, what Charlie had shown me, what he had inspired me to do, was willingly give up some of my wildness, for love. I spent another night in the basement with Charlie, reaching out hourly in the dark to stroke his body, to tell him how much we loved him, to tell him how big his pack was, that it stretched across the continent.

The next day, I ran down to the cabin to do a bit of work and grab a few things to take up to Mike's with me, and as I was on the computer, Eli wandered in the open cabin door. Charlie and Eli hadn't seen each other in a few days, and so when I finished up my work, I scooped up Eli and took him up to Mike's, too. When I walked into the basement with Eli in my arms, Charlie's face lit up and his tail started thwapping the bed from where he lay. I set Eli on the bed beside him, and they spent the afternoon curled up like yin and yang in what was obviously some very special brother time. I left them alone and went upstairs with Mike. I peeked in on them a few hours later and they were lying nose to nose, with their little front paws all intertwined.

Later that evening, Charlie drank water twice without throwing up, a great sign of improvement. Mike and I still administered the lactated ringers, but this time, Mike needed to wear thick leather gloves to keep Charlie still while the IV dripped under his skin. That night, I squeezed into bed with the cat and the coyote, and finally had my first night of real rest since it all began.

The next day, Charlie began eating again. He and Eli and I walked back down to the cabin in the morning and Charlie sat in the grass, watching the birds and the lightening of the land as the sun rose higher above the hills. It took a few days for him to get his strength back, but soon we were back in the rhythm of our long walks, and Parvo seemed so very far away.

Seven

October

By October 1, the roads, the gas station, and the mountain were teeming with pickup trucks with four-wheelers in the back and a flame orange cap on the dashboard. Hunters. During deer and elk season, the population of Ten Sleep doubled, as men in camo filled the bars and campgrounds. Each year, Mike took his allocated time off from Wildlife Services and worked as a hunting guide, and he was booked with hunters every week for the month.

With the influx of trigger-happy tourists, Charlie was in even greater danger and I hid him as best I could in the sagebrush. It had been easy to keep him discreet when he was younger; now, we had to walk deep into

Mike's property to find a spot that was shielded from the road on one side, BLM on another, neighbors on yet another. Charlie's "secret spot" was a secluded edge of the meadow, bordered by a steep arc of land and sheltered with tall sagebrush. Even still, I worried. Acquaintances of Mike's, in town for hunting season, habitually stopped by his house to see him even though he was rarely home. I dreaded that one of them would spot Charlie in the draw and feel they were doing Mike a favor by shooting a coyote off his land. I got a heavy chain and heaved it taut across the driveway whenever I left, securing it around two fence posts with padlocks.

The fact that Charlie had to be tied up and hidden when I was not with him was eating me alive. I worked hard and fast on my Vespa manuscript and photographs for The Daily Coyote in order to free up time to spend with Charlie roaming and playing, and felt guilty even for riding Ranger, for it was time not spent giving Charlie more moments of freedom. The Daily Coyote subscription list had grown, and in late September I had set up a website—a blog—as an archive of Charlie's puppy photos that newcomers to the list had missed. Along with sending out new photos to subscribers, I posted earlier pictures on the blog each morning, one every day.

The daylight hours had decreased dramatically by early October, and a chill, a foreshadowing of winter, accompanied the shorter days. Snow dusted the mountain, and in the valley, nights threatened to drop below freezing as well. With a sigh of gratitude for the months I had enjoyed the convenience, I drained my water heater and toilet and turned off the water leading to the cabin before pipes had any chance to burst. I continued to teach in the early mornings, but now I jogged Charlie down to his hiding spot with flashlight in hand, and scraped away frost from my windshield before leaving for work in the dark. Morning's light spread across the landscape by the time I returned home, but I was back to depending on my woodstove for extra warmth. I built a fire, and gave the cabin the opportunity to heat while I took Charlie on our morning hike.

Over the course of late summer and fall, I had been slowly helping Charlie over his fear of horses. I made a point of riding Ranger past Charlie at his tree, first from a distance, then slowly closer, talking to Charlie the whole time. I sat with Charlie after rides while the scent of horse still lingered on my clothes and skin, and I led Charlie near the horses, gradually, during some of our walks. Eventually, Charlie ventured closer and closer to Ranger of his own accord. Ranger seemed to accept Charlie immediately; he never showed any fear or trepidation when approached by the timid coyote, even allowing Charlie to sniff his feet and ankles. In the first week of October, after sniffing at Ranger's feet and tail, Charlie sat on his haunches right in front of him. Ranger's head was low, level with Charlie, the same size as Charlie's entire body. Ranger yawned a great, gaping horse yawn. Charlie yawned back. Ranger yawned again, and Charlie, still seated nose to nose, yawned a return, and they rallied back and forth, until they each had yawned about eight times. I stood three feet away, mesmerized, holding back my laughter, not wanting to break the spell.

After our walk, I dropped Charlie at his hiding spot in the meadow and returned to the cabin to begin work on some photographs, when Mike stopped by during a rare midday break while the elk were bedded down.

"Need any logs split?" he asked.

I loved chopping wood and Mike knew it, but he liked splitting difficult logs for me to show off, and I saved the densest, knottiest rounds for him, and placed bets on whether he or the log would win. Mike always prevailed. Though, once he finished with the knotty logs, I had to grab the ax from him before he moved to the rest of the pile, taking my fun away.

"Mike," I said, sitting on the chopping stump so he couldn't split any more wood, "I'm so torn up about Charlie having to be tied up all the time . . ." My whole chest got hot just thinking about the subject. "I can't stand it. It's just so wrong."

"Charlie's the only safe coyote in the state," Mike said with a dismissive shrug. "You know keeping him tied up is the only way to keep it that way."

I shook my head.

"He's the luckiest coyote alive, Shreve. He's got the most blessed damn life—never had to work for a meal or drink water from a muddy cow track, he's got the most wonderful companionship, you trek all over these hills with him. Charlie's fine."

"But it's not fair," I argued. "I mean, if you look at it the other way, he's tied up for like eight hours a day."

"You want to set him loose?" Mike asked, with challenge in his tone. "You know that coyote would die of a broken heart if you dropped him off in the hills and left him."

There was nothing for me to say to that. I, too, had realized that Charlie had become so emotionally attached to me and to Mike and to Eli that it would, at that point, have been an act of cruelty to take him into the wild and leave him. Still, it tormented me. There was nothing more important to me, nothing more valuable, than freedom. I felt Charlie's life was being robbed from him; that if I had to be chained I would prefer to die. Charlie deserved freedom and safety, and the bottom line was that he had neither.

. . .

Even steeled after decades of guiding, Mike came home depleted and dejected as his hunters failed to respect the animals, their guns, even him. I learned there was a difference between guys that hunt and the archetype of the hunter, a difference that came down to ego versus respect. As a hunting guide, Mike cared about the hunters and about the money, but more than that, he cared about the animals, the challenge, the thought and sensitivity and toughness that was required. The paying hunters didn't need to embody any of this, and they usually didn't; they paid the guide to be the mind. I had heard the same story from multiple guides—where the guide put his hands on the hunter's shoulders and physically turned him to face the animal he was to shoot. Mike found his hunters the animals, he found them rock or tree braces to shoot from, he set the entire thing up, and the hunter pulled the trigger.

"The only bad thing about guiding, is the hunters," Mike said one evening, leaning up against his pickup talking with me and another guide, drawing laughs from both of us.

"Yeah," said the other guide, "wouldn't it be nice to go out and find the elk and then call the guy on the radio and be like, 'Come on out here an' shoot this sonbitch,' and give 'em your GPS coordinates instead of havin' to lug him around with you all day?"

"This guy today," started Mike, "he's got his fancy expensive gun that he doesn't know how to handle confidently, he crams into the pickup and doesn't pay attention where his barrel is pointing and I'm constantly having to tell him to move his gun out of my face . . . So, finally, after days of this, I find these three deer, right off the road. And we didn't have to hike, because, frankly, he couldn't've, and I set him all up, and he shoots. And the deer he shoots at runs off down the trail. And I look back at him, and see he's already got his gun raised and poised to shoot another! I said, 'Don't even think about shooting another deer,' and he tried to brush it off like, 'Why would it be any big deal? No one would know.' "

The other guide threw his hands in the air, disgusted; they'd all been through this before.

"And I said, 'You don't know if you hit the first deer. What if you did and it ran down the trail and died, and then you killed this one, too? How would you explain that to the butcher or the game warden when you only have one tag?' And he fronted like he understood what I was saying but I think he would've been plum happy to shoot the second deer and never even check out what happened to the first. So I said, 'C'mon, we gotta trail it,' and I walked his ass through the brush trailing this deer. He didn't hit it, there wasn't any blood, but I made him walk for it. And he went home without a deer."

Mike's friend shook his head. "You know, they're stupider than we give 'em credit for."

Mike invited me in after the other guide drove off. I rarely saw him during hunting season, and when we were together, he was distant, distracted, worried about where to find the next elk. He turned on the TV and we sat in silence, and I wondered why I was even there. I absently picked a rifle round from a pile on the counter—Mike always had bullets lying around, pulled out of his pockets and left in piles with loose change—and fiddled with it, drawing on an edge of the phone book with the soft lead tip.

"I wish I knew what you were thinking," I said.

"Ask," he said. "Ask anything."

And with that answer, I knew everything, and my questions disappeared. Was it the way that he said it? That was the thing about Mike—one moment he could make me feel like we were the only two people that existed; in the next, like I didn't exist at all. And it was constantly in flux.

Charlie and I walked the pasture as we did every evening at dusk, then I tied him outside the cabin where he could watch the stars come out before I brought him in for the night. Eli came home around nine p.m., ready to lounge and relax a bit before his late-night prowl, but Charlie followed him in and danced around him in excitement, nipping the air to the left and right of Eli's face. Eli stretched out on the floor in the center of the cabin and gave Charlie a heavy-lidded look that said, *Little brother, I am not in the mood. Go away.* Charlie was never one to take such brushoffs personally, and he kept at it, prancing around, hoping Eli would play. Eli was getting visibly irritated, and gave Charlie a meow that said, *What part of "Go Away" didn't you understand?* It fell on deaf ears. Finally, Eli had had it, reached up, and gave Charlie a good bite on the tail. Charlie leapt straight onto the bed in what may have been the first time a cat treed a coyote. Charlie stood on the bed and picked an old leather glove out of the toy bowl that sat on the table at the end of the bed, and began tossing it in the air and shaking it about. One toss sent the glove sailing over the edge of the bed and it landed on the floor next to Eli, who remained lying there comfortably. Charlie crouched at the edge of the bed with his chin on his paws, his gaze shifting between the glove and the cat with alternating looks of longing and nervousness. I had been watching from the kitchen, making tea, and I burst into laughter. "Are you too scared of the cat to go down and get your glove, Charlie?" I laughed, and stooped down to toss the glove back to Charlie. Eli was still boss.

My laptop computer had a video camera built into it, and after a few hectic mornings trying to get my truck to start—it had no heater, no defrost, and refused to budge during cold spells—and returning to an ice-cold cabin after work when the woodstove had gone out, I presented a plea to my managers to teach from home, thereby making life easier for me in the winter, and also freeing up office space for other teachers. They agreed. On my way home from my last morning at the office, I swung by the post office, picked up a few days' worth of mail, and flipped through it as I drove home, glancing up to see the readerboard had changed. *"Spiritual Body Mass,"* flashed the sign, as I drove by holding an envelope with familiar handwriting from my past.

It was a letter from Linda, my boss from the job I had as a teenager, and to whom I have remained very close. I grew up on an island in the Puget Sound, a half-hour ferry ride from Seattle, Washington. In the ten years since I had moved away, the population of the island had nearly doubled, and with the population growth had come a great deal of construction and development. Fields and wooded areas I wandered as a child were cleared, banks of town houses in their place. Enclosed with Linda's letter was a lengthy clipping from my hometown newspaper about coyotes. According to the article, "Missing Cat" posters had become ubiquitous on the island, and residents were divided on how to deal with the growing presence of coyotes in their midst. Some wanted the coyotes left completely alone, others wanted them completely gone. One man, interviewed for the article, stated that he was so concerned for the safety of neighborhood children and pets, he was driven to go outside and shoot his gun in the dark to "scare the coyotes" on nights he heard them howling.

The article expressed the dilemma the island was facing, one that was becoming common across the country as coyotes held an ever-growing presence in urban and suburban areas. I understood the desire to protect one's pets and possessions, and I also understood the desire to live and let live. But neither side held the answer for me. I was learning that coexisting with nature in all its wild forms is one of the gifts and lessons of this life, one that takes flexibility and creativity on our part.

Coyotes are as clever and as driven as any human, and are simply adapting as people pave their world. The article inspired me to write a letter to the editor of my hometown paper, sharing my experience with Charlie and my belief that a solution had more to do with individual choices, and a consciousness regarding our personal choices. Do people really need five-thousand-square-foot homes? As long as they are being built, as long as subdivisions continue to spread, animals will be displaced.

Teaching from home was an enormous convenience. On cold mornings I was able to keep the fire stoked between students, I didn't have to worry about my truck failing to start as temperatures dropped, and I didn't worry quite as much about Charlie, since I was on the property. One mid-October morning, Charlie and I went out on our walk after I finished teaching; it was one of those strange October days that often show up halfway through hunting season, so unseasonably hot it can spoil meat before hunters have a chance to get their game out of the field. Even so, hunters were out; I heard gunshots throughout the BLM and kept Charlie close to me. Instead of venturing far into public land as we had been, we wandered the property and didn't cross the fence line into BLM.

I tied Charlie at his secret spot in the meadow buffered by sagebrush, made sure he had water, and went up to the cabin to work. The Daily Coyote blog had been gaining popularity on the internet, separate from the subscribers. It had been nominated for a Weblog award, and traffic to the blog had increased from about thirty hits a day to a few hundred in less than a month. Suddenly, I was jolted from work by the sound of a gunshot. Loud. Close. Too close. I tucked my feet in flip-flops and took off out the door. I ran down the driveway and down the draw, sprinting though I felt like fear had stopped my heart and kept me from drawing a full breath. Oblivious to the scrapes across my feet from the sagebrush and cactus, I raced to the spot where I had left Charlie, ran harder, scanning the area for him. I saw him in the shade of the cut. He was lying on his belly and elbows, watching me run toward him with a calm and perplexed expression. I took a deep breath, and it gave me the oxygen to keep running, past Charlie, to the fence line.

Three men in orange vests walked the top of a draw, not twenty yards from Mike's fence. "Hey," I called out. They either ignored me or didn't hear me and dropped down into the draw. I jumped the fence and kept running until I crested a ridge and could see them moving away from me. "Hey," I yelled again. *"Hey!"* The men stopped. One of them turned and started toward me, and I dropped to a walk to catch my breath.

"Hi," I said when we met. "I know you guys are on BLM right now, and that's fine, I just heard a shot from my cabin that was just so close, I had to see what was going on."

"Yeah," the man said, "it's deer season, you know."

"Yes, I do know," I said, trying to hide my irritation. "But there are three houses, there, there, and there, and I want to make sure you know these are property lines."

While it is illegal for a person to shoot an animal on private land, even if they are standing on public land when they take the shot, the law is not always respected. And I wanted to keep them away from Charlie.

"Good luck," I said as I turned away, and thankfully, my presence proved to be enough to get them moving farther out.

"Were you afraid, running out there by yourself?" Gloria asked when I told her the story.

"Afraid for myself?" I asked with a laugh. "No! I was just mad. I mean, these guys had a hundred thousand acres of BLM to hunt, and yet they chose to walk fence lines and shoot their guns in a triangle of land between three houses." But I thought about why I was so mad, because technically, they had done nothing wrong. "You know," I said to Gloria, "I haven't fully relaxed since Charlie came into my life, just knowing he could be killed at any time. I guess I took it out on them." We laughed. "But really," I said, "who would want to hunt along fence lines, anyway?"

Mike called on his way down the mountain. His hunter had gotten an elk and they were headed to the corrals if I wanted to see it. Since Charlie was skittish around strangers and the thought of keeping his jaws away from a freshly dead elk seemed an unfair task for both of us, I left him under his tree. As I walked to the corrals, I smiled to myself as I watched Charlie racing back and forth under the tree, gathering his scattered toys. One by one, he grabbed them and put them in a pile–an old baseball hat, a leather glove, a bleached rib bone. Then, once they were gathered together, he took each item in his jaw, moved it five feet away, and created a new pile.

Down at the corrals, Mike and his hunter had hung the enormous bull elk from the hay forks of Mike's backhoe and were in the process of skinning it. Even with the hind hooves raised ten feet in the air, the elk's head rested gently on its side in the dirt. Mike introduced the hunter and me. I remarked on his bull, then watched as Mike finished skinning. He swept his knife swiftly and deftly between hide and muscle, peeling back the skin, preparing the animal for the butcher. When Mike reached the front legs, he yanked down hard on the hide to peel it from the upper leg, then sliced the tendons around the knee and broke the joint, so that the entire hide separated from the elk in one piece, with all four lower legs still attached to the hide.

The hunter was only interested in the rack and the meat, and Mike left the hide in a clump as they carefully maneuvered the elk into the back of the pickup and wrapped it in a clean tarp.

"We're gonna run to Hyattville to the processors," Mike said. "Do you want to ride along?"

I smiled but declined, and eyeing the discarded hide, directed a question to the hunter. "Would you mind," I asked, "if I took the elk legs there, if you don't want them?"

He looked at me kind of funny, but didn't ask why and I didn't offer.

"Sure," he said. "Go right ahead."

"Thanks!" I said, and with a grin to Mike, asked to borrow his pocketknife. I dug the legs out from the pile and cut them free. The legs were each longer than my own forearm, twice as thick, and still warm, pliant in my hand. They were coated in dense, chocolate brown hair, the raw knee bone exposed at one end and the other ending in a heavy black hoof. I stacked three of the legs on a high shelf to return for later, waved my goodbyes as Mike and his hunter headed for Hyattville, and started back to Charlie with an elk leg in my hands.

"Charlie," I sang as I neared his tree. "I have something for you . . ." Charlie flattened on his belly in the tall, brittle autumn grass, waiting for me to approach, but upon noticing—either by sight or by scent—what I held, he leapt up and bounded toward me, springing into the air and trying to snatch the elk leg out of my hands, his eyes lit with desire. I held the elk leg to shoulder level. "Charlie, sit," I said firmly. He planted himself on the ground immediately. "Good job!" I praised, and offered him the elk leg, presenting it with both hands. Charlie hopped to his feet and placed his jaws carefully around the center of the leg. It was heavier than he expected, the weight uneven in his jaws, and he tipped sideways, refusing to let go of the leg. He put a paw on the leg

and gently let go, rearranged his hold, and then resumed a trot, carrying the elk leg proudly in his mouth. After several regal passes, Charlie settled down in the grass and began to gnaw on it, lost in contentment.

Upon hearing Charlie's reaction to the elk leg, Mike began bringing home the hearts and livers of his hunters' game, which usually were left behind with the entrails. It took four days to psych myself up enough to pull the first heart out of the cooler, place it on my cutting board, and slice it into pieces. Elk hearts are about the size of a teakettle, and I had vivid mental images of blood spurting everywhere when I first cut into it. Yet I found the heart is a dense, solid muscle, and there was no blood at all. When I fed Charlie part of the heart, he entered a state of rapturous delight. I had never seen him quite so blissed out on food. I gave some to Eli as well, who ate it but was more interested in the daily ground meat. And so I saved the hearts for Charlie, for special times and treats. "Next year," I said to Mike, "I'm putting up a sign that says 'Hunters, I Want Your Hearts.'" He laughed. "You'd better clarify," he said, "or they'll be lining up at the gate."

That night, I got ready to go to bed and brought Charlie inside, but Charlie wasn't interested in being in the cabin yet, as had become common on nights leading up to a full moon. The moonlight was bright enough to make shadows and animals stayed alert and active because it was so light. I had gone on horseback rides at midnight or on long walks with Charlie, no flashlight required. Inside, Charlie took a quick spin around the perimeter of the cabin, then squeezed past me to face the door, rubbing the length of his body against the woodstove in his eagerness to return outside. The smell of burning hair wafted up from his dense coat; it had been filling in, getting full and plush for winter, and was thick enough that Charlie didn't notice the heat off the cast iron. "Charlie!" I said, exasperated, "you're burning," and I lifted his hind end to pivot him away from the stove. A patch of fur about the size of my palm was singed, the ends of the hairs curled, but noticeable only by the rough texture, and not really by sight. I clipped him to his rope and let him out again. On the nights around a full moon, I was used to waking up between midnight and one to let him back inside; by that time he was ready to hop up on the bed and sleep.

As I was drifting to sleep, my mind filled with images of Charlie's face, baring his teeth, and then him in a hunkered pose, running and whimpering. I wrote it off as bizarre paranoia and fell asleep. I woke at midnight, slipped on moccasins and a jacket, and went outside to bring Charlie in. The night was clear, the moon bright enough to see his furry form curled up in the dirt behind the cabin. I hurried over to him; the October air was cold on my legs and I was eager to bring him inside and jump back into bed. I smelled skunk on the air–though I had not seen it, I had noticed its odor around the cabin for a few days and had gotten a live trap from Mike, a large metal box with a trip-release door. If an animal entered, the door dropped down behind it, but the animal remained unharmed. I baited the trap with cat food and a chicken egg and set it fifteen feet from the corner of the cabin, but the skunk had not wandered in, nor had Eli.

Charlie hopped to his feet, his tail wagging, and beelined to the open door of the cabin. I jogged back behind him, unclipped him from his rope at the door, and Charlie dashed inside and was curled up on the bed before I had closed the door behind me. "You're sure ready to be in here," I said to him as I crossed the cabin to nuzzle his head. Now the smell of skunk was overwhelming, horribly strong inside the cabin. Dread, mixed with a bit of panic, seized me. Had the skunk crept in while I was out getting Charlie and sprayed inside the cabin? Or worse, was it still in the cabin? Charlie had not taken his eyes off me; he seemed needier than usual, and so I continued to the bed to pet and kiss him. When I bent down to nestle my face between his velvet ears, I nearly passed out. He had been sprayed.

I did not want to send Charlie back outside. Skunks are commonly infected with rabies and I had never been able to vaccinate Charlie. I crawled into bed with Charlie curled up at my feet and tried to sleep, tried to withstand the awful, penetrating odor, but within minutes I was nauseous from the smell. Reluctantly, I went to the door and cooed to Charlie to lure him back outside, clipped him back onto his rope, and left him to spend his first full night outside alone. I opened the window even though it was 28 degrees that night in an attempt to air out the cabin, and tried to sleep.

The next morning, I went out to check on the banished coyote. Charlie was desperate to be near me and wanted to nuzzle against me, and though it was a pitiful sight to be confronted by, I kept him at bay; the odor of skunk gave me an instant headache and I had to teach. I held my breath and ran Charlie down to his tree, and after my three hours of teaching, I ran down to the gas station mini mart for tomato juice.

"Feelin' healthy?" Lynn, the cashier, asked.

"No." I laughed. "Charlie got hit by a skunk last night!"

Lynn was one of the few locals who had seen Charlie, once, while he was sitting in the passenger seat of my truck when I had stopped for gas during one of our summer drives. She had been both entranced and frightened by the sight of him in my truck, by being in such close proximity to a coyote, by the wild that was undeniable in his eyes. This was the common reaction, I had found, from all who had seen Charlie—be it a man or a woman, a hunter or a rancher's wife. Regardless of their opinion of coyotes, all were genuinely curious, held in some small way by the mystery of Charlie before them.

"Do I reek?" I asked Lynn, for the smell had burned into my nose over the last ten hours.

"Nope. I couldn't tell at all!"

With the two bottles of tomato juice tucked under my arm, Charlie and I ran up to Mike's empty house for a bath. I tied Charlie to one of the support poles outside the basement door, wrapping his leash tightly around the beam so there was not much slack or room for him to move. I filled a bowl with warm, sudsy water, found a pair of rubber gloves to wear, and began to bathe Charlie's face and neck. Charlie, who was already feeling nervous and neglected, did not cooperate. He danced away from the soapy water and snapped at my hands. I could understand, given the night he'd had and my refusal to give him much attention that morning. I went back into the basement and put on a thick leather glove, then a heavy quilted glove over that, and thus protected, returned to Charlie and simply let him bite my hand. I grasped his lower jaw to keep him steady while I poured both bottles of tomato juice straight over his head, chest, and back.

I felt awful but Charlie seemed unfazed. When it was over he shook himself and licked the tomato juice from his legs. I stripped off the gloves, my hand unaffected by Charlie's jaws, cleaned up our mess, and we set out for a long walk to dispel any leftover tension. "Now, if only it would rain," I said to Charlie as we ran down a steep red bank, for even a brief rain would rinse Charlie down and wash away the odor of skunk that hung in the air around the cabin. To my delight, just as we headed in from our hike, the rain began. I left Charlie in the draw under his tamarisk tree, and by early afternoon, what smell remained in his fur was dull enough for him to join me inside, curl up, and get cozy.

Eight

At nearly seven months, Charlie struck a prominent silhouette in the moonlight. It was the beginning of November and the moon, though waning, was still full enough to cast shadows; bright enough to write by, bright enough for someone on the road to spot the form of a coyote in my driveway. I lay awake, still and tense in my bed. I couldn't determine if I had extremely low expectations of people–because I didn't put it past someone driving by to stop in the road and shoot Charlie in the night, even if they knew, as most of the townspeople did, that he lived with me; or actually quite high ones, that someone who didn't know about Charlie might see a coyote in a driveway and, not knowing he belonged there, shoot him out of protection for the residents of the cabin nearby.

I finally tiptoed out into the chilly night, brought Charlie in, and crawled back into bed. Charlie jumped on the bed but seeing I wasn't going to play, jumped back over my head and down the stool stair, back to the door, and scratched to go out. I ignored him. Charlie scratched more urgently; I could hear his nails tearing the Styrofoam that lined the cabin door. He didn't relent; he was determined to go back outside. Reluctantly, I turned on the light and groaned under my breath when I saw flecks of broken Styrofoam covering a three-foot area around the door. I clipped his leash to his collar, the other end still tied outside the cabin, and Charlie bounded out the door. I tried to relax, to pull away from the worry of him being seen, and eventually drifted off, but slept lightly and woke two hours later to a strange noise on the porch. I turned on the outside lights and peered out the door. When Eli came home in the middle of the night, he signaled he wanted to come in by jumping into the window box and meowing until I woke up. Now Charlie was halfway up the woodpile, on his way to the window box.

The next morning, before dawn's light reached the sky, the first snow of the season drifted down into the valley in soft flakes as large as down feathers. The hunters had gone; the land was quiet. After teaching, Charlie and I went down to frolic in the meadow where I let him run unhindered, top speed, the leash still clipped to his collar but trailing behind him. There was always a sliver of a chance that Charlie could take off after a rabbit, and the trailing leash was my only chance of catching up to him and getting him off the road or out of a neighbor's yard if it ever came to that. Charlie didn't mind. He tore out across the meadow, galloping through the snow, the crystal flakes kicking up behind him, glittering through the air. Charlie lowered his head and buried his snout in the snow as he ran, and when he lifted his head in a gleeful toss, a little dome of snow balanced on his nose.

The oval meadow was bordered naturally on all sides by steep rising banks up to the driveway to the north, by the hill to the corrals to the south and east, and by a natural shelf to the west toward the cabin. When Charlie reached an edge of the meadow in a dead run, he zagged to the left, turning on a dime. His grin widened and he dashed a few more high-speed Z's around snow-laden sagebrush and then, his tail bouncing behind him, raced straight back to me, eyes shining, ears folded back so far that they were invisible from the front. Our connection had continued to deepen; it felt like a partnership that grew stronger between us all the time. It was the opposite of what I had expected with Charlie—I had thought he would get more distant as he grew up. Instead, our communication had reached a level that amazed me, that seemed to be based more in telepathy than verbal commands. Charlie understood he was allowed to run free in the meadow, and he never tested the boundaries; he stayed inside the perimeter on his own accord, and since I could trust him, I could allow him this wonderful freedom.

I loved watching Charlie run at full speed, witnessing the awesome athletics he was capable of but rarely got to use. As Charlie raced away from me, I darted behind a giant sagebrush and peered through the branches at Charlie's receding body. He looked like a rabbit when he ran through the snow, propelling himself forward with both back legs at once. Charlie spun around and looked startled when he saw I was not standing in the place I had been, but in a moment he knew the game was on and ran even faster, even happier, toward the giant sagebrush where I hid. Charlie leaned into a curve and dashed behind me, playfully nipping my calf on his way by. "Tag!" He streaked off, ran halfway across the meadow and plowed to a stop behind a clump of tall grass, dropping to his front elbows in the classic canine play stance, his furry butt high in the air, tail wagging in anticipation. I jumped out from behind the tree and jogged through the snow toward him. "Where are

you?" I sang as I got near. His tail wagged and he wiggled in his hiding spot. I pounced around the clump of grass where he crouched, reaching out to rub his flank in the moments before he tore out running. Out into the meadow we went, Charlie loping through the snow while I ran after him; he loved being chased. He spun, changed his course in attempts to dodge me, racing away, looking back over his shoulder at me with a grin as I did all I could to keep up with him, to keep the chase.

We heard the familiar barking of Mike's dogs down the road, and saw his truck come into view and take the turn up the driveway. The barking crescendoed as the truck crossed the cattle guard, and Charlie, who had been standing still and alert, started pacing and yipping in high, punctuated bursts. The dogs continued to bark as Mike drove up the hill above us and Charlie arched his neck back in a deep, slow howl. "Aroooooo . . ." he howled in answer to Mike's dogs. I stifled my adoring laughter–I couldn't help but smile on the rare occasions that Charlie howled and didn't want to distract him from it with any noise from me. His mouth formed a perfect loose O and his ears lay back, flat against his neck as he shared his song. Charlie was a quiet coyote for the most part; he never answered other coyotes we heard in the hills and only howled in response to Mike's barking dogs, Eli's insistent meows, and the times that I howled to him myself. He had only recently become vocal and still seemed a bit insecure about it; half the time, his howl began tentatively, then became full and strong, then wavered out again, and his expression seemed to say, *Why? Why does this noise come out of me when all I try to do is purr?*

Mike sat idling in the driveway above us, and as his dogs settled down, Charlie quieted as well. Mike leaned over to unroll the passenger window and wave.

"Did you hear it?" I called up to him.

"Yeah!" he said. "Hey, Chuck," he called down to Charlie, and revved his truck, which set his dogs to barking again.

Legs planted wide, Charlie lifted his head once more in a low howl.

Mike beamed. "You comin' up later?" he asked.

"Yeah," I said. "We'll be up."

Charlie and I walked back to the cabin, but about twenty feet from the door, Charlie stopped and refused to continue forward. I looked at him, trying to figure out what was causing such a reaction. Charlie stared at my truck as if he had never seen it before, obviously afraid to walk past it. I looked at my truck. It was parked where it was always parked; all that had changed was that there was now three inches of snow layered upon hood, roof, and bumper, apparently change enough to make Charlie wary. I let Charlie take his time, and only after much slow and cautious investigation did he deem it safe enough to trot past.

Inside the cabin, Charlie and I roughhoused on the bed. Though he could saw through a one-inch-wide by one-eighth-inch thick leather strap in four seconds—I timed it once—he always kept it gentle with me; though he was feisty enough to keep me on my toes. He had figured out how to open the refrigerator, and would empty it, too, if given the opportunity. After barricading the refrigerator door for a week, I went to Worland and bought a door latch that I fastened to the fridge to lock it. And I had to be careful what I kept in my pockets, for Charlie found it hilarious to stick his long snout in my coat pockets, grab whatever I had, be it notes or lip balm or pens, and race away so that I chased him.

Charlie curled up to nap while I worked on a calendar of Daily Coyote photos I was putting together to sell on the website and just after dark, we walked up the hill to Mike's house. Snow piled thick on the long, curving driveway, reflecting enough of the moon's light that I didn't need a flashlight. Charlie frolicked the whole way up, oblivious to the cold, while I stayed cozy in wool leggings, a wool sweater, wool jacket, down gloves, silk scarf, a hat, and snow boots.

"Hi, Mike," I called as we walked in. Mike came out from the kitchen with a smile and a kiss for me, his blue eyes sparkling, and a rub for Charlie, who fell on the floor at Mike's feet, rolled over, and gazed at him with adoration. The house smelled divine. "I'm building us dinner," Mike said. "Just greasy potatoes, and I found a couple steaks from the calf I butchered." I was salivating already. Mike made potatoes like no other—thinly sliced and fried in oil with bacon and onions.

Charlie squirmed loose and made an exploratory round through the house, sniffing at everything, looking like he wanted to move in all directions at once. Mike's oldest dog, Jake, spent much of his time inside now that the weather was getting so cold. Jake was nineteen, and had spent his life hunting coyotes with Mike. His left ear was half gone where it had been ripped off by a coyote, and he had torn up his share of coyotes in return. Jake was the alpha in Mike's pack; he still bluffed the other dogs with his barks and snarls even though he hobbled feebly and his movements more closely resembled a rocking horse's than a virile canine's. Jake and Charlie had never really met during the summer. Jake was usually off somewhere alone or sleeping in the chicken house, but tonight, Jake was inside.

Charlie scampered into the living room and Jake, who had been stretched out on the floor, heard the dainty clatter of Charlie's toenails on the wood floor and lifted his head. When he eyeballed Charlie, he lurched up with a booming woof. Charlie, full of benign curiosity, pranced over to Jake with his neck stretched out and low, sniffing the air between them, looking at Jake with innocent eyes. Jake curled his lips to show all his teeth, teeth that were broken and yellow and worn down from age, and growled seriously, growled from his belly. Charlie reached in closer, his feet planted but his body stretched forward as far as it could. Jake snapped at the air and lunged toward Charlie, barking loudly with promises of death, but his lunge was slow motion; Jake was the equivalent of an old, old man and moved like it, and Charlie darted away. Jake stood staring in the direction Charlie ran, barking his warnings into the air. Charlie ran out of the living room, around the staircase, and back into the living room from the other side. He scampered up behind Jake, who was still focused and barking in the other direction, and nipped his rump. Jake's bark grew deafening in outrage, and he managed to turn himself in a tight circle to face Charlie's retreating tail. Jake looked over to where Mike and I were standing, watching the whole thing, with a look to Mike that said, *Do you know there's a coyote in the house?* He hobbled determinedly in the direction Charlie had run. Charlie, meanwhile, had trotted around the staircase once again—he was loving this; it was a game to him—and again crept up behind Jake. This time, Charlie pulled up his toenails as he got close so that he traveled silently on his paw pads. Another quick nip to Jake's rump and Charlie was off and running, leaving Jake booming another series of barks in his wake.

There were times Jake managed to turn fast enough to surprise Charlie, and both their feet slid and scrambled on the wood floor before they could get their footing and it looked like they were going to end up on top of each other, but they never did. Charlie could have killed Jake, he was quick and capable enough, but he didn't even want to hurt him; it was just a game. Yet he knew enough to stay out of Jake's reach so that it never turned into a fight, taunting him from a distance and sneaking in for a playful nip.

"You'd think Jake would smell Charlie on you and me and figure it out," I said to Mike, for Jake was an incredibly loving and gentle dog to Mike and to me.

"No," Mike said. "That ol' dog's been fighting coyotes for eighteen years. I don't think he'll ever learn to like Charlie."

We stayed the night at Mike's house. Charlie curled up at the foot of the bed, nestled between my legs and Mike's. In the morning, Charlie woke when we did, and wiggled up between us to lick our faces, so soft and sweet, his tail gently thudding against the bedspread. I turned to Mike. "Can you believe you have a coyote nuzzling you in bed like this?" I asked.

"No," he said, "I can't."

The snow melted as abruptly as it had arrived; such was the pattern in early winter. It snowed, then melted off, back and forth for over a month, and it wasn't until late December that the snow stacked up on the ground. Mike had five tons of corn delivered to supplement his cows over the winter. He was out, so I met the delivery truck at the corrals and watched in awe as the driver unlatched a wooden panel at the back of the truck and a mountain of golden kernels poured out. Charlie and I often wandered around the corrals on our walks, and a few days later, after Charlie sniffed around the corn and deemed it nonthreatening, he sprang into the air and dove headfirst into the pile. With ears laid back and a fanatical grin across his face, Charlie dug to the bottom of the pile, the loose corn filling in around his legs as fast as he could dig. He flung his head up suddenly, and bounded across the pile with kernels flying, stabbing his long snout deep into the corn until he began to dig again, corn showering out behind him. Then he stopped and looked around for a moment before launching into an elaborate series of leaps and inspired coyote acrobatics in the midst of the corn pile. I jumped in the corn pile myself. I loved the sensation, heavy and liquid-like, as thousands of kernels conformed around my body. The corn pile became a daily stop during our walks, and Charlie was so happy, so hilarious, so full of joy as he played in it, that I was inspired to coin a new phrase, "happier than a coyote in a corn pile," which Mike and I promptly adopted to replace "pigs in shit."

As we were spending more time down at the corrals, Charlie became curious, then intrigued, by the calves that were being held in one half of the corrals while they were weaned. He ventured to the pole fence and peered beneath it, studying the dark forms of the five-hundred-pound calves. The calves, though large, betrayed their youth with their own innocent curiosity, and a few ventured toward the fence when they caught sight of Charlie. Charlie darted back and stood four feet away, staring at the calves against the fence, then ventured closer, slowly, tentatively.

As Charlie neared, the calves hopped back in nervousness, but then, like Charlie, were drawn back in, and after a few rounds back-and-forth, Charlie and the calves stood nose to nose with only the pole fence between them. I kept hold of Charlie's leash so that he did not have room to duck under the fence and enter the corrals, because I was not sure what might ensue and I did not want him getting trampled. But Charlie reached up slowly to the nearest calf, sniffed the air twice, and gently let out his tongue to lick the broad, shiny nose of the calf. Both calf and coyote seemed surprised, and hopped slightly back, but almost immediately moved back together, and Charlie gave the calf another gentle lick. Nearby calves began pushing toward Charlie and they lined up in a neat row along the fence, and Charlie proceeded to prance up and down the row, licking each calf flat across the top of its nose.

A week into November, Mike and I went to Worland together to do errands, and we took Charlie along for the ride. Mike had gone out at the

very end of hunting season, after his hunters were gone, and gotten an elk himself, and now, along with the usual grocery and hardware stops, Mike's elk meat was ready to be picked up from the processor. Charlie jumped in Mike's pickup easily and eagerly, knowing it well by sight and sound and scent, and settled between us, sitting poised with his chest proud, looking straight out the windshield. Mike and I wondered how he would react to oncoming cars on the highway, as he was so frightened of strange vehicles. Yet Charlie was unfazed, as if he sensed he was untouchable, in a protected bubble where other cars and trucks were no threat.

Once we reached Worland, things changed slightly. The highway between Ten Sleep and Worland is fairly desolate, nothing but badlands to each horizon and very few cars or trucks. Worland is a small town by most standards—a main drag less than ten blocks long, a handful of stoplights—but the buildings lining the street and the traffic around us along with the accompanying noise seemed to overwhelm Charlie, and he became a bit anxious and tired, and curled up on the bench seat to avoid it. The most startling part of our trip was being witness to people's reaction to Charlie, or lack thereof. Mike and I stopped at the A&W for milkshakes, and when the girl brought them out to the truck, she looked at Mike and then across the length of the truck to me, offering small talk as she handed us our shakes, oblivious to the coyote between us. Even though Charlie sat on the seat between us with his ears perked high, she simply didn't register him. We then stopped for gas, and the gas station was jammed with cars and trucks waiting for pumps. Of all the people who sat idle, waiting, only one woman noticed Charlie, and it was evident in her face. She ended up pumping gas adjacent to Mike and asked, incredulously, "Is that a coyote?" It was a bizarre phenomenon, proof of the adage that people see what they expect—or don't see what they don't expect.

I was thrilled to have elk again; the elk that was left in the freezer was years old and only fit for a coyote. When we got back to Mike's, I thawed two steaks and cooked them. They smelled divine, but when I bit into one, the meat was like rubber, and seemed to get even tougher the longer I chewed it. It was so tough that I fed mine to Charlie instead. The bull Mike had shot was so large that the base of each antler was bigger around than my calf. The bigger the antlers, the older the bull; and the older the bull, the tougher the meat. Yet we now had a freezer full of this tough old elk. Determined to enjoy it, I got out my favorite stew recipe the next day and switched in elk for beef. The long, slow-simmering elk created a delicious stew, which Mike and I ate for a week straight, though Mike picked out the carrots and celery, being a diehard meat-and-potatoes man.

By mid-November, Charlie and I were spending nearly every night at Mike's, and we all loved the new arrangement. While it was a little difficult for me to be away from the cabin so significantly, things between Mike and me felt easy and connected, and it was far safer for Charlie than down near the road. I loved the stimulation Charlie had from Mike's dogs and from all of us being together. Mike was happy we were up there, too; he stopped asking if I was coming up and started expecting it. Even Eli had picked up on the change, and when Charlie and I set out afoot in the evenings, Eli scurried out the cabin door and walked up to Mike's with us. When we got there, Eli dashed inside and halfway up the stairs to avoid Mike's dogs, three of which now spent the nights inside, and settled comfortably on a hand-hewn log stair where he was out of reach and could survey everything. I stretched out on the sofa while Charlie jumped in Mike's lap and covered his face in licks. With a fire crackling in the fireplace and the snow swirling outside, and three dogs and a coyote and a cat and Mike and me all piled into the house together, we all felt wrapped in a feeling of love and safety and company.

Eli had been lean through the summer, but suddenly had transformed himself with layers of fat and thick fur for winter. One evening, I was upstairs reading on Mike's bed with Eli curled up beside me when Charlie bounded up the stairs and onto the bed with us. He stood over Eli, nuzzling and nibbling Eli's face and back. Eli rolled over onto his back and pawed at Charlie's head while Charlie danced over him with ears folded back and tail wagging. In his excitement over requited attention from the cat, Charlie opened his jaws and put Eli's entire head into his mouth. Eli lay on the bed, unfazed by Charlie's jaws wrapped around his head, though after several moments he seemed to get annoyed, and with one meow, Charlie let go and instead, mouthed the air around Eli's head. Eli, by now, was now fully awake from his nap and feeling feisty, and he launched himself into the air and took a swat at Charlie's head. Charlie leapt off the bed with Eli in hot pursuit. Charlie ran to the far end of the bedroom and turned on his heel when he reached the wall; Eli bounded after him with his tail straight in the air. Charlie jumped back up on the bed and, with a quick look over his shoulder, saw Eli jump on the bed after him. Down he went off the other side with Eli on his tail, and off they ran, screeching in tight circles around the bedroom. Mike heard the racket of their feet and my laughter. "What is going on up there?" he called up from the living room. "Eli's chasing Charlie!" I answered. "It's the funniest thing ever!"

Once Eli started following us up to Mike's, I brought his litter box up; the layout of Mike's deck and the other dogs made it difficult to let Eli and Charlie outside to do their thing. During an earlier storm, Jake, subject to the incontinence of old age, had peed on the floor in the kitchen, and though Mike had cleaned the area with bleach water, Charlie smelled the event and assumed the kitchen was the designated bathroom area. I took to carrying a Tupperware with me at all times so that if Charlie started to squat, I could dash over and catch his pee in the Tupperware, often before any hit the floor. But this was a bad pattern to start, and meant I never fully relaxed, being on constant pee alert, and something had to change.

One evening I was in the downstairs bathroom brushing my teeth and Charlie came wandering in to see what I was doing. He sniffed around the sink and the shower, and on a whim I opened the shower door for Charlie, to see what he would do. Charlie sniffed the edge and hopped into the shower itself. I turned on a trickle of water, thinking he might find it interesting, but instead of playing with the water, Charlie squatted in the shower and peed down the drain. When he was done, he turned a tight circle and hopped out as if it were the most natural thing in the world. I burst out laughing and hugged him and praised him, then turned the shower on full blast to flush it.

The next morning when we all woke up, I ran downstairs with Charlie on my heels and opened the shower door for him. Charlie hopped in, peed, and ran to the living room to tell the other dogs good morning. I kept up this ritual, leading Charlie into the bathroom in the morning and evening, and within days, Charlie had turned it into habit.

One evening when we arrived at Mike's, there was a ziplock bag of homemade jerky on the coffee table, and Charlie grabbed the bag and made a run for it. Mike ran to head him off and I followed behind Charlie to block a retreat. Charlie spotted Mike in front of him and turned to go back the other way, where he saw me. When he realized he was cornered, he lowered his body down and reached out his neck to set the bag on the floor between us and just waited there. Charlie liked to test authority, but always acquiesced when he was called on it.

Mike and I drove to Worland to spend Thanksgiving with Mike's extended family; it was the first time I met most of them. It was a full and happy house, everyone friendly, the meal delicious. Still, after a few hours Mike and I looked at each other with an identical expression—we were both itching to get home to Charlie. Soon after Mike's parents left to make the drive back to Cody, we excused ourselves and left laden with leftovers. We drove back to Ten Sleep, holding hands the whole way, and as we turned up toward home, the headlights illuminated a new message on the readerboard, *"God's Living Bones."* Back at Mike's, we fed Charlie bits of leftover ham and turkey until he began hiding pieces in the flowerpots for later. Smiling at his antics and at each other, we slipped into bed and gave thanks for each other while Charlie slept curled up at the foot.

On the last day of November, I was at my computer midmorning, working on photos for The Daily Coyote. When I finished up, I checked my email, and sat in puzzled curiosity as dozens of emails began to flood in. My inbox counter rose: 15 . . . 23 . . . 35 . . . 60 . . . 77. Seventy-seven messages since I had last checked my email two hours earlier. *What is going on?* I thought, as I moved my cursor to open the first one. I read several; each one was praise for The Daily Coyote blog. *What is going on?* I wondered again, and logged in to my site meter, which tracked the number of visitors to the blog along with any websites that referred visitors to my site. The last five hundred referrals all listed the same site, dooce.com, one of the most popular blogs on the internet. I clicked onto it. The woman who wrote dooce had posted a link to The Daily Coyote on her site, and I had gotten more hits in one hour than I had in the last month.

Nine

At the end of the first week of December, the thermometer dropped to negative 14 degrees. I was back to spending more of my time at the cabin—I had so many emails to answer and new subscriptions to add every day before I sent out the morning's photo, and the only way I could take care of the work I had was if I spent the night at the cabin rather than at Mike's. The fire in my woodstove had gone out in the night and when I woke, it was below zero inside the cabin. It was impossible to take a deep breath; the icy air inside my lungs made me cough and burned in my chest. I stayed warm with layers piled on the bed—flannel sheets, an electric blanket, a down comforter with a thick flannel duvet cover, and a heavy, king-size wool blanket I doubled in half over the top of it all, and Charlie and Eli curled side by side in the wool next to me.

I kept wool leggings and a fleece shirt in bed with me under the covers, which I put on while still in bed. I had quickly found that dressing in clothes that had been sitting out in the frigid ambient temperature was a painful endeavor, and made it a practice to hang my bra and jeans near the woodstove to warm before I put them on. Still, I had to psych myself up for several minutes, buried in the warmth of soft layers and body heat, before launching myself out of bed, though Charlie and Eli remained curled in tight balls on the bed. I shoved my feet in Uggs and knelt before the woodstove to get a fire going. I placed two small logs in a V in the stove, shoved crumpled paper in the space between them and laid kindling across the top, then lit an edge of paper with a match. I watched as the kindling caught and flames wrapped around the underside of each log. Once the flames took hold, I could throw on a dense pine log full of pitch and the heat would begin.

After a few mornings of waking up to freezing temperatures inside the cabin, I learned to fill my teakettle with water before going to bed; that way, I could put the ice-filled kettle directly on the woodstove to heat rather than having to wait for my jugs of water to thaw before making coffee and washing my face. After it had sat for a few minutes on the stove, I shook the teakettle and heard water slosh inside—the ice had melted, and I poured a bit of water into a shot glass and returned the kettle to the woodstove to boil. I brushed my teeth with this one cubic inch of water, pouring small amounts over my toothbrush to moisten it and spitting into a mason jar that functioned as my sink, which I emptied out over the layers of sawdust and wood-chopping detritus beyond the cabin when it got close to full. The teakettle began rattling, a signal the water was the perfect temperature to douse a washcloth and wash my face. The clean, damp heat on my face was one of the simple joys of morning. I rubbed in moisturizer, donned a hat and scarf because it was still cold inside, and by then, the water was boiling for coffee.

Honey does strange things at temperatures around and below freezing. I bought honey by the gallon and couldn't drink coffee without it, though I left the bulk jar at Mike's house and refilled a pint jar to keep at the cabin. If I forgot to set the honey jar on a stump beside the woodstove to warm while the water boiled, I was left to carve out jagged flakes with a butter knife to melt in my coffee. By the time I had my sweet coffee in hand, the animals were stirring. Eli looked up but saw no reason to move from his cozy spot, while Charlie, whose coat would keep him warm to temperatures of minus thirty degrees, yawned, stood on the bed in a deep stretch, and then bounded straight for the door.

When I reached in to clip on his leash, Charlie curled his lip and snapped at my hand. I whipped my hand away, stood tall, and told him to sit. He sat, but when I reached in again with the leash, he pounced to his feet and snapped at my hand again. I gave him a mild glare, annoyed, confused, and a little distraught. For the previous few nights, when I had gotten up to let Eli in, Charlie had rumbled a low growl when I got back in bed. The first time it happened, I was so surprised I thought I had woken him from a bad dream, then wrote it off as him being a grump when it happened again. But it was becoming consistent, and he was suddenly showing aggression with the leash as well. Half the time, I clipped his leash on without incident, as had always been the case. But other times, Charlie snapped at my hand, never actually biting me, but sending a definite warning. He was telling me something, but I didn't quite know what.

I went to the fridge and got a small piece of cheese. Sometimes, holding the cheese over his head distracted him long enough for me to tuck in with my other hand and clip the leash to his collar. As I moved toward Charlie, he began growling, more of a low, croaking noise than a dog's growl, and when I got within inches of him he snapped at me with his lightning jaws again. "Sit, Charlie," I said. It amazed me that even when he was croaking like a frog, even when he was snapping at me, he sat immediately when I asked. But the moment I moved toward him with the leash, he was on his feet with teeth bared, though he never came toward me. I took a step toward him and he snarled and ran around the ladder to the loft, returning immediately to the door as he obviously wanted to go out. I made sure not to corner him against the door, not knowing if he'd try to defend himself against me if he had nowhere to run. And so we circled the ladder, our quick turns punctuated with croaks from Charlie, pleas from me, until Charlie was panting and I was sweating and we were both so worn out, we simply stopped. It was like fighting with a person for so long you both forget what the fight was about and it all just dissolves. I asked Charlie to sit. I reached out my hand and pet his head. I offered him the cheese again, and as he reached up for it with his teeth, I reached under his jaw and clipped on his leash.

I let Charlie out to sniff the frigid air and stuffed another log into the woodstove. The pitchy pine was throwing white flames and the cabin had warmed up enough to start my computer. In the past week, The Daily Coyote had taken off like a wildfire. After the link from dooce, I was being linked across the internet and was getting tens of thousands of hits a day, as many as 125,000 page views in one day. It was surreal, and the exposure brought with it the strange phenomenon of notoriety, something I had never wanted. Hundreds of sites and internet forums were actively discussing Charlie, my blog, and my character. Much of the commentary was touching and filled me with a sense of accomplishment; James Wolcott wrote a post on the *Vanity Fair* website that I wanted to have embossed in gold leaf and hang on my wall. But there was also a fair amount of criticism and debate over what

I was doing. Some people declared that it was illegal to keep a wild animal, even though it was easy enough to learn, through Wyoming Game and Fish, that it was not; others declared that it was all about my ego, even though they had never met me.

After scouring the latest crop of referring websites via my site meter and sending out the daily photo to the rapidly growing subscription list, I tore myself away from the internet and put on jeans, long johns, a wool sweater, and my old down jacket, the nylon patched with duct tape where I had absentmindedly burned several holes in it on the woodstove. I was having a selfish flare-up. It was painfully cold outside and all I wanted to do was stay cozy and try to catch up on the hundreds of emails and dozens of orders that had come in over the past week, but Charlie needed a walk, deserved a walk. There were times I felt my life was governed by Charlie and his needs, though I was sure when Charlie had a day of difficult behavior, similar feelings were coursing through his veins: *Why must I accommodate myself for you? I'm made to run wild with no one to answer to . . .*

I was still tormented by the hours he had to spend tied up, and I was certain this was causing frustration in Charlie as well. I wished I had mountain land with a locked gate and could put up a ten-foot fence around one square mile. But even though work had been going well and the website was bringing in a burst of income thanks to new subscribers and calendar orders, I didn't yet have enough for a coyote-safe fence near the cabin. Even if I had, the ground was frozen solid, impossible to dig. I swallowed the last of my coffee and headed out the door for the morning hike.

I had untied Charlie to jog down the draw when Charlie stopped in his tracks and stared down the hill across the street. A coyote, a twin of Charlie, same size, same coloring, was standing just on the other side of the road. It had stopped broadside, and was staring back at us. My eyes

flickered between Charlie and the coyote across the street. In his eight months of life, Charlie had heard coyotes often and never paid them any attention, but this was the first coyote he had seen face-to-face and I wondered what he would do—would he run to it? Was the experience as surreal to him as it was to me, to see an animal, nearly identical to himself, twenty yards away? Neither coyote moved, and then, for no apparent reason, Charlie darted over to me and stood behind my legs like a shy child. At Charlie's movement, the other coyote trotted off into the horse pasture, looking back only once.

Charlie and I walked hard and fast up and down the frozen draws. The red dirt was solid as ice, deceiving, for it still held the contours and visual sign of crumbly clay. It was easy to turn an ankle or lose one's footing on the steep, frozen draws. But it was gorgeous—crystals coated every branch, every remaining stalk of grass, every gnarled sagebrush, like a million tiny mirrors. Charlie was unfazed by the cold but I had to keep moving at a quick pace to stay warm. The balaclava that covered most of my face stiffened as my breath froze and crystallized on the fabric as we trekked. After an hour of traversing the hillsides, I took Charlie down to his hiding spot and went back to the cabin to see what was going on with the internet. I couldn't stay away from my site meter, couldn't keep from reading what was being written about me across the internet, and I took it all so personally. I was getting hundreds of emails a day, and they were either so heartfelt or so judgmental that I felt I had to respond, though in the time it took to answer one, five more came in. Even when I was out on walks with Charlie, the parts of my days that had always been solely about being in the land with him, my mind was on the internet, wondering about statistics, comments, orders, emails—it was thrilling and sordid and it was consuming me. And when Charlie was in the cabin with me, I hunted through my cupboards for toys to give to Charlie as a way of buying time; I was overwhelmed, and resorted to giving Charlie gifts instead of attention.

We spent that night at Mike's, but even there, Charlie growled at me in bed and stood over me, his paws on either side of my chest. Mike reached over and pushed him off, and Charlie settled down at the foot of the bed. I was puzzled by Charlie's inconsistent behavior. Was he simply being a teenager, testing boundaries and power? Was it hormonal, the surge before February's mating season? Was he growing up and his wildness taking hold? Or was he reflecting the new stress I was feeling?

The next day, I did some online research on dogs that growled in bed. I learned it was a common display of aggression, and that keeping an aggressive dog off the bed was key in restructuring their behavior and asserting one's alpha status over the dog. I had no way to keep Charlie off the bed in the cabin. The cabin was one small room, and if Charlie was inside, he had access to the bed. Now that we were spending more time back at the cabin, I was racked with guilt over Charlie losing the stimulation of being with Mike's dogs, and with fear of him being spotted from the road when he was hanging out alone outside the cabin. All these factors led me to decide that Charlie should move up to Mike's house.

December 12, the night Swedish pagans considered the longest of the year, was the first night Charlie and I spent apart since the one night in May. I prepared Charlie's dinner in Mike's kitchen and left as the two of them lounged in Mike's living room where a fire blazed in the fireplace, and walked down to the cabin in the early darkness of deep winter. I was incredibly sad. Eli was waiting in the window box and he slinked into the cabin with me. I sat on the footstool in front of the woodstove to stoke up the fire, watching the flames dance, blue at the edges, golden inside. I fiddled with a stick of kindling, letting it burn in my hands. I had heard if one is ever lost, the first thing to do is build a fire for companionship. Warmth is secondary. Eli jumped up onto my shoulders like a parrot and crouched there purring.

I called Mike first thing in the morning.

"How's Charlie? How was the night?" I asked.

"He's fine, it was fine," Mike said, as if nothing were out of the ordinary. "I'm just sittin' here sipping coffee and he scratched at the door to go out, so he's out in the snow roughhousing with Pita."

"OK," I said. I didn't know what else to say; I felt a little empty. "What are you doing today?"

"I'm set to fly," Mike said. "I've got to get those coyotes out back. I'll be leaving here shortly to meet the plane when the sun gets up."

A group of coyotes were living in the BLM directly behind Mike's house. Though the coyotes weren't harming anything, they were situated between two sheep areas and were close to a subdivision. Their voices carried when they sang, and people had been complaining, and some of the local guys were running around on four-wheelers with their rifles, looking for the coyotes to shoot.

A few hours later when I finished my morning's work on the computer, I walked up to Mike's to take Charlie for a hike. The raw sound of an engine grew louder and closer. A small, fixed-wing plane appeared from over the hill and flew right over me. It was Mike and the pilot. The day was gorgeous—sunny and blue skies, and snowing a light glitter of flakes at the same time. Charlie was tied in Mike's yard and ran up to me as I neared. I untied him and together we sat on the steps of Mike's deck as I rubbed his body. I could see the plane clearly—it was not four hundred yards away, making its first circle over the coyotes. The plane tilted and dove into a deep banked curve; I gasped as it swooped down to just a hundred feet above the ground. *BOOM-BOOM-BOOM*, Mike's shotgun rang out and echoed across the draws. The plane veered upward and flew into the sky, circled, and dipped into another dive toward land. *Boom-BOOM*. More shots rang out. I sat on the step sobbing, my arm around Charlie, knowing that each blast from Mike's shotgun was another dead coyote, the coyotes I had heard singing together earlier that morning. Inside, I screamed, *No, NO,* but there was nothing I could do and I couldn't take my eyes off the tiny blue-and-white plane, diving and rising against the blue-and-white land, the engine roaring in acceleration as it pulled the plane back into the sky and leveled out toward the horizon.

Charlie and I made a large loop of the property following the BLM fence, hiking up the hill and walking the ridge toward the road, then dropping down to the corrals. We circled back up through the horse pasture, then ended up back at Mike's empty house. I grabbed a few logs and Charlie and I went inside, and after I fed the fire, I chased Charlie around Mike's staircase, through the living room and dining room, out into the hallway and around again. Charlie, thrilled at being chased, scampered away with his tongue flapping, looking over his shoulder back at me with sparkling eyes to make sure I was still running behind him. Once I was dizzy and Charlie was panting through his grin, I got him a bowl of water in the kitchen and decided to make a treat. Deep winter and approaching holidays inspired me to bake, something I rarely did anymore.

I always joked that Charlie was a gluten-free coyote. If Mike gave him a bit of cheeseburger, Charlie ate the meat and the cheese and left the bun; he licked the jam off toast and left the bread; he even went so far as to pull the breading off fried chicken and eat only the meat. He never ate cookies or rolls that Mike offered him. While Charlie lounged on the floor at my feet, I made a few batches of gluten-free scones and cookies, eager to sample them; I hadn't had a cookie in about eight months. Charlie, who always wanted to try anything that anyone was eating even if he ended up spitting it out onto the floor, sat before me and I gave him a corner of my scone. Charlie gobbled it up, and sat again, asking for more. I gave him a bit of a cookie and he devoured that as well—hard proof that he was officially a gluten-free coyote.

When I returned to the cabin, over a hundred emails were waiting for me. Four of them were from publishers. I was astounded. I had never seriously considered writing a book about Charlie, but here were four editors interested in such a book. I called my agent in New York and told her of the developments of the past two weeks and the interest from editors. She told me to forward the emails to her and asked if I could get a proposal together within a week. *That's impossible,* I thought to myself, but said, "I'll do it." I quit my teaching job, which was a difficult choice, but I no longer had time and I was making ample income from web orders. I sat down to write a twenty-page book proposal in five days.

That night, I went outside to refill my water jug from the hose that ran to the horse trough. The sun had set but the horizon still had light glowing behind it from far away, and the thinnest sliver of moon shone above me as I crouched in the snow. It was so quiet, so real. An owl hooted nearby; I missed Charlie so much, but he and Mike were having fun together and I could see the simple happiness Charlie brought Mike; it was a good thing for both of them. Knowing this was a balm for my longing.

The next day, I ran to Worland to pick up a batch of Charlie calendars from the printer's. I almost missed the new message on the church readerboard in my hurry to get home: *"Risking Discipleship."* I drove straight up to Mike's to take Charlie on a hike before filling the latest orders and getting them to the post office. Charlie was lying in the weeds beside the fence. I walked up to him and reached out to pet him. Charlie lurched to his feet and before I knew what was happening, his teeth were bared and he had my outstretched hand clamped in his jaws. Biting hard, he shook his head in the classic death shake. Stunned from the action and the pain, I yanked my hand away from him, turned on my heel and walked straight to my truck, pulled out of Charlie's line of sight, and burst into tears. It was hard to catch my breath, I was crying so hard from shock and pain and betrayal and confusion. I have no idea how long I sat there with my hand cradled in my lap, sobbing with my forehead against the steering wheel, but I was jolted from it when Mike returned home and pulled up beside me. His face was worried.

"What's wrong?" he asked. "You okay? Charlie okay?"

I couldn't speak but saw panic take over his face.

"He bit me," I managed to get out between tears.

"You okay?" Mike asked again.

I nodded. I was wearing a thick wool sweater with cuffs that were too long for me, and so even when I folded them twice, the cuffs covered my hands to my knuckles. The layers of wool had provided a cushion and Charlie's teeth had not punctured me, but the bite bruised my hand deep inside, and for days I couldn't open a ziplock bag, put my hair in a ponytail, or use my thumb at all.

The next day, the wind blew across the surface of the snow, sending it furling like dry ice as I walked up to Mike's. I missed Charlie. As I approached, I saw Charlie relaxed and happy, running to Mike and rolling over, playing with all the dogs. I realized I was scared of him. I couldn't understand what had prompted the bite; I hadn't noticed any warning signs. It was one more outburst against me, like the growling, like the difficulty with the leash, and I believed, intuitively, that it had something to do with me. I have always felt, as painful as it might be in the moment, that whatever entered my life was there largely because of

me, and though other people or events might play a part, I could never put blame, or even cause, solely outside myself. The sight of Charlie frolicking with Mike and the dogs upheld my theory. Charlie hadn't once shown any aggressive tendencies toward the dogs or to Eli, and he remained totally submissive to Mike.

Mike saw me coming across the hill and tied Charlie to the fence. I hopped over the fence farther down and walked a wide arc around Charlie, trying to look like I had a determined goal and not like I was shying away from him in fear. The dogs bounded in the house as we went inside. I sat on the stone hearth in front of the fire and Jake eased down at my feet. I couldn't bear to leave Charlie outside by himself.

"Will you bring him in, Mike?" I asked. "Please? I have to see what's going on sometime, anyway."

"OK," Mike said, "but keep Jake near you." A brilliant idea. Even though Jake was old and crippled, he was mightily determined to keep Charlie away from himself and his people, and his bark always sent Charlie back a few steps.

The faces of animals gazed down at me. A ram in one corner; two mule deer as different from each other as could possibly be on the main wall, an exquisite elk centered between them. Their stoic, unerring gazes didn't come from glass eyes; they seemed to stare right at me, inside me, knowing and not judging, impassive but not indifferent, allowing me to feel who I was in that moment; stopping time for me to feel it, as time has stopped for them eternally. Charlie was eager to come in and raced up the stairs and down again, and pranced around the edges of the living room. He looked me in the eyes and sniffed the floor around Jake before Jake sent him back to the edges. I couldn't stay. I was too afraid, and though I did not know a lot, I knew that projecting that kind of energy would just set me, and my relationship with Charlie, back even further.

I called Mike before I went to bed to check on Charlie and ended up in tears. I had just watched a video I had made of Charlie and Eli in the cabin with me; Charlie was bouncing around, happy and carefree, then he and Eli ate together out of a pot on the kitchen floor. I had filmed the video three weeks before but it seemed so far away.

"It feels like a lifetime ago, that we were like that," I said, heartbroken.

"It's probably just hormones, with mating season right around the corner," Mike said. "Think of him as a cowboy sittin' in the bar at two in the morning, and he can't find a woman so he just wants to fight. That's all it is. It'll be okay."

I didn't totally believe him but couldn't help but burst out laughing through my tears.

The next day, well aware of my new fear and my desire to overcome it, Mike presented me with a deerskin tunic. It was something he had worn years earlier, and it was simple and gorgeous. It was honey-colored deerskin cut like a pullover shirt, with a slit at the neck and a row of five-inch fringe on the back across the shoulder blades. Made by one of Mike's neighbors, the hem was just the natural edge of the hide, and all the seams were hand-stiched with leather laces.

"Charlie can't get his teeth through this leather," Mike said as he handed it to me.

"It's gorgeous!" I was blown away by the beauty and simplicity of the item and of his thought. And so I armored up, with the hopes that I could project confidence instead of fear if I was no longer worrying about my bodily safety.

I prepared to take Charlie on a walk, the first walk since he had bitten me. I wore a wool sweater under the deerskin tunic; the combination provided both padding and protection, and it was incredibly fluid, comfortable, and warm. The leather cut the wind and cold yet allowed for easy movement and range of motion. I was certain no modern coat had ever improved on the Native American design. I also wore padded welding gloves, jeans, my heavy leather chaps, and snow boots. I knew Charlie would be hard-pressed to hurt me with this attire. I knew I could not hold fear in myself; not being afraid was key. But it was hard, because I was afraid.

Running up and down the draws with a coyote was one thing; hiking through six inches of snow while wearing fifteen pounds of leather was quite another. The chaps were cumbersome, but they did allow me to stretch out on my side in the snow and stay completely warm and dry while Charlie dug to the earth or sniffed intriguing sagebrush. They also made quite a difference in the cold air, though it wasn't that my legs felt particularly warm, just that comparatively, my butt, clothed only in denim, was frozen. Charlie had a blast, scooping up snow in his lower jaw as he raced through the pasture, returning upon occasion to rub his head against my leg. For that hour and a half, everything seemed good again, but I couldn't forget my fear.

When we got back, Mike was home. I stripped off my boots and chaps, and took off my sweater because it was warm in Mike's house but put the deerskin tunic back on. I watched Charlie climb into Mike's lap, roll over for him, lick his face. I was glad the two of them could share that, and that Charlie felt so comfortable with Mike, but I was heartbroken, and jealous deep inside. I was the one who took Charlie on walks morning and night; I was the one who made sure he had food and water.

I was starting to wonder what I needed to do to get my relationship with Charlie back in order, if Mike was wrong, if it was not purely hormonal. If it was hormones, wouldn't his outbursts show up in his other

interactions? He remained at the bottom of the totem pole with Mike's dogs, and he never questioned or challenged Mike's dominance. There was a reason Charlie was only taking it out on me. Mike supposed it was because I was female. I wondered if it was something less obvious. Mike had his four dogs to demonstrate his alpha status, and he also had an air about him; whatever his reservations were regarding most people, Mike simply did not fear animals. He had once strangled a mountain lion with nothing but his bare hands and a piece of baling twine. I, on the other hand, had always considered Charlie and me more of a team than as having a relationship based on rank. In fact, I had made it a point not to own him, and to coexist without ever being the boss of him. I didn't know the answer that would lead me to a solution, but I knew this deeper probing would lead me to the correct question.

Charlie was looking more like an adult—his coat was getting thick and full, his muscles defined. "Look how buff his shoulders are," I said to Mike as Charlie stood between us, getting petted from both sides. Mike raised his eyebrows back at me. "Yeah," he said. "I noticed that." Apart from his full, round body, Charlie was becoming more angular as well; pointy ears and nose, and points of fur thick at his cheeks. His paws were arrow-shaped at the end of his long legs when one looked down at them, and even his balls were pointy. They were shaped like teardrops, round on one end and pointed on the other, and they were growing, too.

A week before Christmas, Mike's younger daughter, Kadi, returned home from college. I always enjoyed it when she came to visit—we talked about music and clothes and the dramas of the college sophomore. Charlie was out in the yard when Kadi arrived, and he watched her walk back and forth as she unloaded her car and brought her suitcases into the house. When Charlie came in later that evening, he sniffed nervously at Kadi's belongings, a suitcase in the hallway, a sweatshirt flung across a chair, and ran up the stairs to watch from above. When he came down, he kept to the edges of the rooms. He huffed at her, a nervous bluff that made him sound tough, but he did not approach her. Kadi ignored Charlie for the most part and acted like sharing a house with a coyote was no big deal. She was intrigued by him, but did not stare at him or fawn over him, which in retrospect probably made her seem like an alpha figure in Charlie's eyes.

Kadi called me at the cabin the next morning to invite me along to the mountain; she and Mike were going up to find a Christmas tree. I bowed out because I felt picking out a Christmas tree was an intimate family activity, one that was even more special for her and Mike to share alone as this was just the second year they had had a Christmas tree since Tracy's death. I told her I'd be up in the evening to help her decorate it. When I got up to Mike's house, Kadi had bins of decorations open and white lights and tinsel spread across the living room floor. I brought up some tree ornaments as well, a box of small crocheted Santas my grandmother had made. While Mike worked on college paperwork for Kadi on one side of the room, Kadi and I wound lights around the tree and filled it with decorations. We wrapped gold beads around the banister of the stairs and draped them over the two huge antique bear traps Mike had on his mantel, and even decorated the houseplants with the ornaments that didn't fit on the tree.

I dreaded that Charlie would either be terrified of the tree, or do something insane like grab a branch in his teeth and pull the entire thing down, but when he ran in the door, he sniffed the tree a few times, did the coyote equivalent of shrugging his shoulders, and ran off to find some old ham he had buried in a flowerpot. He could not, however, resist the ornaments for long. He snuck up to the tree and, with the tips of his teeth, gently pulled off the crocheted Santa ornaments within his reach and dropped them on the floor. He only went for the crocheted ornaments, and he didn't chew them up or run off with them or ever disturb the tree itself; he just deliberately plucked them off, one by one, and left them below the tree.

Later in the week, I ran to town to pick up another calendar order and brought back a bag of marshmallows for Mike and Kadi and me to roast in the fireplace. Kadi whittled a point on a long piece of kindling for a roasting stick, and I had a marshmallow skewered on the end of a long knife.

"So," I said, "these are celebratory marshmallows . . ."

Mike looked at me, curious. He had seen how hard and fast I had worked on the book proposal and had been eager to hear how the blog had grown, truly amazed by the series of events of the last three weeks.

"I got a book deal today," I said, and told them the details of the deal and how I had six months, starting then and there, to write the book. Mike and Kadi were thrilled, and I was too, but I was overwhelmed; it all happened so fast.

As I pulled my long knife from the fire, Charlie came over wanting to sample a marshmallow himself. He patiently sat in front of me as I peeled the golden outer layer off with my teeth. I pulled the remaining inner glob off the knife tip and offered it to Charlie. He folded his ears back on his head, reached forward and licked at it delicately, then took the gooey nub from my fingers. It stuck to his upper lip, to the side of his muzzle. Charlie ran over to the doormat with the marshmallow stuck on his face and rubbed it off with his paw. The three of us watched him, giggling, as he gobbled it up off the floor and trotted back for more.

* * *

As the last day of the year approached, Charlie and I went on a long walk and ended up at one of our old spots, the meadow where we played tag. As we trotted down the path, all our old games came flooding back from my memory, and evidently, the same thing happened in Charlie, because suddenly, we were back in it, both of us running and grinning like the old days, free and fun. All the fear and animosity and whatever else had plagued us vanished, and we were the way we had always been. I scooped up a handful of snow—it had finally warmed enough to pack snowballs—and I tossed it out beyond Charlie. It landed with a faint thud and left a crater in the snowbank. Charlie, ears pricked, raced over to where it landed and with his teeth, dug the snowball out from the snow surrounding it, holding it, perfectly intact, in his mouth. I laughed as he trotted back to me with the snowball in his mouth and bent down to form another. I threw it far, and Charlie dashed through the snow to retrieve it. It seemed we would never tire of this game.

On our way home, we ran into Mike coming in from work and the moment he pulled up alongside us, something switched in Charlie and he jumped up with his front paws on my hip and started growling. "Go," I said to Mike, "Just go and I'll see you back at the house." My heart was beating faster, but more than scared, I was sad. I looked down at Charlie and made a low, serious growl in my own throat. Charlie stepped back, and we returned to Mike's without incident.

Late that afternoon, Mike and I jumped in his truck to go feed his cows. They were off the mountain and recently back in his pasture. Every day, as would be required until May, we loaded, by hand, nearly a ton of hay into the back of his pickup to feed the cows. We drove into the frozen pasture, where I jumped out of the cab and climbed to the top of the hay to begin my job. Throwing hay to the cows relieved my every mood; I felt a certain peace on the back of the truck, wobbling across the frozen manure piles. My only focus was the quick satisfaction of the baling twine popping under my knife blade as I broke apart the bales, flaking off a quarter bale at a time, each section falling from the truck to the icy ground with a satisfying thud. The cows eagerly, greedily followed the truck, nosing and shoving one another's heavy black bodies in attempts to get closer to the truck, each cow hoping to spot the richest, most delectable flake of hay to devour. I gathered the yellow baling twine in my fist, working fast and methodically. The hay had to be spread evenly so that each cow got her own portion, but I had to be sure to drop enough hay at a time so that it did not get trampled and wasted or blown away in the wind. The rhythm and purpose of the task grounded me, invigorated me, distracted me from the worries swirling in my mind, and whatever the weather, I was happy and at peace atop the hay truck in the beautiful, harsh land.

On the drive home, I burst into tears spontaneously, tears of despair and sadness over Charlie: over what, to me, felt like the greatest loss. I couldn't trust him, couldn't help him, couldn't be with him. Sometimes I knew Charlie was happy and content with the new arrangement; sometimes I knew he wasn't. And equally as distressing was that I didn't know how to fix it. I still didn't understand why his behavior had changed, and why it was so inconsistent. Mike tried to keep a positive front but I knew he was concerned—not for Charlie, but for my safety. I turned my face to the window so Mike wouldn't see me crying. "Are your eyes sweatin' again?" Mike asked gently.

Ten

In early January, alone in Mike's house, I sat in front of the fire trying to pinpoint when everything changed. Mike was at work, Charlie was outside in the yard. In November, Charlie and I had been at the peak of our relationship. I could confidently control him without the leash and we shared an incredible connection and understanding. Now, I never knew if or when Charlie would snarl, jump on me, or worse. I had been researching canine aggression online and discovered Cesar Millan, also known as The Dog Whisperer. I had heard of his TV show but had never seen it, and I immediately ordered his most recent book, *Be the Pack Leader*. It had just arrived and I was hooked the second page in. More than providing a step-by-step solution, Millan discussed the role of a person's attitude, and how this, in tandem with particular action, was what really turned difficult and heartbreaking situations around.

Canines are happy to be followers; there is less mental stress involved, and order brings them a sense of peace. However, if they sense leadership is faltering, they will take it upon themselves to become the dominant figure to fill the void. In their mind, someone must be the boss or chaos is imminent. Millan's book was based on the premise that if a human can assume the role of the alpha, a dog's behavior can be drastically changed—because the dog chooses to change.

I thought back carefully, going over events and dates, and realized with a sharp intake of breath that the dynamics between Charlie and me changed almost the very moment The Daily Coyote got so popular and I got so stressed. Finally, it all made sense to me. If Charlie was looking to me as the alpha, and then, being so sensitive as animals are, he perceived my feelings of overwhelm and distraction, he then naturally took it upon himself to step in and take on the role of alpha himself. I had put together the puzzle and it made me so unbelievably sad, but it also made me hopeful that we could get our relationship back.

Charlie was asking me to get a handle on things, asking me to fully come into my own power, and his behavior showed me my inconsistencies, showed me where I was still weak. I laughed; I thought I was so tough. I had bucked every authority my entire life, rode a Vespa across the country, moved to Ten Sleep sight unseen, but I was weak in the ways I deferred to others. I needed to learn how to hold my own—always, with everyone—not to prove anything, but to be authentic. This went beyond the dynamics between Charlie and me. This stretched into every realm of life. And then the tears really began, for I suddenly recognized all the ways I had set myself aside to be with Mike.

I had to become more self-aware than ever in order to overcome whatever anxiety might creep in; to identify what I really was thinking about at all times and how I felt about it. It was essential that I not let stress about my work take hold while I was with Charlie, even if that was just an hour at a time throughout the day, so that he could begin to feel that he could depend on me. I decided then and there to stop checking my site meter, and to no longer read anything that was being written about me or Charlie.

It dawned on me, while Mike and I were loading hay the next afternoon, that my concern about the rift between Charlie and me—the apparent loss—was similar to the way I felt about Eli when Charlie arrived at the cabin, when Eli had stayed away much of the time. Yet in spite of that trying month, Eli remained a solid, grounding, loyal part of my life. This gave me another nudge toward faith, that Charlie and I could work through the difficulties and get to a better place.

Mike was close friends with a man named Mark—Mark, who was "Moustache" from the day I first met Mike on the road. Mike and Mark had known each other since they were nineteen. Mark lived in the southern part of Wyoming and was a fourth-generation cattle rancher, but he also spent two months of each winter living at Mike's and guiding hunters in the Bighorns, looking for mountain lions. Mark arrived in the first week of January, tall, dark, brawny, and loud. His first night at Mike's, we brought Charlie inside in the evening. Charlie was wary, and huffed at Mark, but overall, he reacted similarly to how he had with Kadi. Charlie kept a fair distance from Mark and never let Mark get close to him, but generally went about things as he always had, climbing on Mike's lap and racing up the stairs and tormenting Jake. Mark couldn't get over how "like a dog" Charlie was. Over and over, he exclaimed what had become common to Mike and me. When Charlie ran in the house, Mark said,

"He wags his tail, just like a dog!" When I sat in front of the fire rubbing Charlie's belly, Mark, from the couch, proclaimed in amazement, "He likes to be scratched, just like a dog!" But Mark didn't forget he was a coyote. Before I left to go back down to the cabin, Mike and I gave Mark bits of cheese to offer Charlie, to see if Charlie would get close to him. Charlie slowly crept in, his eyes on Mark's face. As he dipped in quickly to take the cheese delicately from Mark's fingertips, I hid my face to stifle my laughter, as it was clear the lion hunter was nervous, afraid that Charlie might take his whole hand instead of just the offered cheese.

That night, I curled up in the loft of the cabin with the Dog Whisperer book and reread a sentence in which Millan listed the four great traits of dogs: honesty, integrity, consistency, loyalty. I lay back; I'd always had the first two, honesty and integrity, as part of my character to a fault, but I had never maintained consistency, not if my life depended on it, and I realized I had never been loyal to anyone but myself.

In trying to regain a trusting relationship with Charlie, I had to learn more about him, learn what he was communicating with his body language. I studied his ear and tail positions, began to decipher the patterns, become fluent in their messages, and it led to insights about myself. I didn't know I was so coyote. But it was there, in me, part of me, from the very beginning. The loner, running for myself and by myself; dipping into company when the occasion presented itself but not needing a pack; adaptable to any environment; excruciatingly sensitive, with difficulty trusting until after thorough investigation and even then, reserving absolute trust. Surviving, exploring, assimilating; lashing out; also, feeling pure joy and nothing but. Taunting others because they were old and stuck and I could see that, and, at times, deferring to those around me out of self-protection but not necessarily respect. Happy to sit and observe; a little pushy when I wanted something. Desiring, most of all, to bring smiles to those around me and also very honest introspection, and with that, power. Real power, the power of the individual—which I then realized did not mean being an island, that this life is a kaleidoscope and the most wondrous designs are created when different shapes and colors interact together, and when they overlap, light passes through both.

The Dog Whisperer's consistent, trademark advice was to project "calm assertive energy." This, essentially, is an absolute confidence that can be perceived by everyone around and by canines in particular. Once, months before, Mike and I had had a conversation about fear. I told him I thought the opposite of fear is love, and Mike had said he believed the opposite of fear is confidence. I think we were each half right, that the answer is a combination of love and confidence, for love keeps confidence from turning to pride, and confidence keeps love from becoming a doormat.

The next day, I took a break from work and went with Mike to try to find a lost calf on the mountain. The snow was thigh deep, and the only way we could get to the upper meadows was on a borrowed snow machine. I had never been on a snowmobile before. Mike drove, and I sat behind him, gripping his body with my thighs while my arms reached behind me to keep the sixty-five-pound bale of hay we brought up for the calf balanced on the tiny rack behind me. Even at fifty miles an hour, even around windy turns, even lacking the ability to hold on to Mike with my arms, I was totally confident in Mike's ability, totally confident in my safety, and I could relax and enjoy the thrill of the ride. I'd been on the back of a motorcycle with a driver I didn't trust—who didn't feel stable or adept—and been a passenger in a car with a bad driver, and I remembered that feeling, remembered what it did to me—the panic and overwhelming desire to step in and take over. It drove the point home of everything that had gone on between Charlie and me—I felt out of control, and overwhelmed by the demands of the internet and keeping up with my blog, and that was precisely when Charlie stepped in and decided to be the boss. Gliding across the snowy mountain with Mike, I took in the sights of snow-laden trees flashing by, felt the contours of the land beneath us, happy to have Mike as "alpha snow-machine driver." I needed to provide this for Charlie, to give Charlie the opportunity to feel happy and relaxed once again, while I took control and became the calm, assertive, capable leader.

According to the Dog Whisperer's book, there were major benefits to leading a dog on dedicated, purposeful walks as opposed to general wanderings dictated by the canine, which was how Charlie and I had usually traveled. With resolve to try out Millan's philosophy, I led Charlie out the back gate behind Mike's house and into the BLM where there was an old two-track road half-overgrown with sagebrush. A few inches of snow covered the ground and the trail snaked out before us, a clear ribbon of white. I kept Charlie on the trail—this was the goal, this was our path for the day. When Charlie veered toward the bordering sagebrush, I said, "Hey," a term we used often and which meant, *You're not doing what I'm asking you to do,* and simply stood still with the leash held taut but never pulling him, until Charlie took up down the trail. Charlie understood quickly what was being asked of him and we walked easily beneath the blue sky. After about a mile, we turned back and followed the trail home again. Charlie was exhausted when we got back to Mike's, more so than usual. He flopped down in a sunny spot in the yard and I bent down, forehead to forehead, to kiss his long snout. My face fit perfectly between Charlie's long ears, and their softness framed my cheeks as I nuzzled into the downy fur of the crown of his head. He gently rolled onto his side as I stroked his body, his underfur dense and warm, heated in the sunlight. The Dog Whisperer was obviously correct, that dedicated walks stimulate an animal's mind as well as his body, and are therefore more exhausting.

. . .

It had become more difficult to take photos for the daily emails—not only did my walks with Charlie require more work and awareness from me so I couldn't focus on photography, I still wore the deerskin tunic and thick padded gloves, and the gloves hindered my ability with a camera. Plus, with Charlie at Mike's, I didn't have as many opportunities to take pictures. It was frustrating, but it was one more stress that I had to let go of while I was with Charlie, and find ways to become even more creative with the time we had together to get a supply of good photos.

Though I stopped reading about The Daily Coyote on other websites and forums, debates still raged in the comments section of my blog, and I was still getting hammered with emails. Criticism, advice, and directives came in from every direction and on every topic—why wasn't Eli neutered, Charlie shouldn't have a collar, Charlie should have a more visible collar, on and on, as well as demeaning criticisms of me personally, of my character and my motives. I didn't understand why people felt the need, or the right, to be so judgmental about an animal and a person they had never met. When I told Mike about the online drama, his response was, "You can't fix stupid, but you can delete it," but that wasn't easy for me; it took a few months for me to reach the point where such comments no longer affected me. But what did have an immediate and lasting effect was that by being on the receiving end of such a deluge of judgmental thought, I learned just how ridiculous it is to judge others in any capacity. Coming from a notoriously judgmental family, I had both rebelled against being told what to do while simultaneously adopting that attitude toward others, without even realizing how often I told people what I thought they should do because I was overlaying my own opinions and experiences on their lives. It's so egotistical to believe that we know more about someone else's reality than they do, and such a waste of time. I was glad to be shown the mirror so blatantly, and be

given, in this way, the opportunity to recognize this behavior in myself and then drop it from my repertoire.

One benefit that came with the phenomenon of the internet was the connection and support I felt when I was contacted by two women—who lived two thousand miles apart and did not know each other–who had raised coyotes themselves. One woman had raised multiple coyotes and coydogs that had since passed away; the other was still living with the twelve-year-old coyote she and her husband had raised from when it was just weeks old. I was thrilled to get emails of introduction from these women, and felt lucky to be able to draw on their knowledge. I immediately emailed them both with a description of Charlie's recent aggression. One woman shared her own experience, a similar display from the coyote toward her but not her husband, one that took a heartbreaking year to mend. The other woman suggested strict training, in small doses several times a day, to establish my authority. Both of them told me to never back down or run away, and to never hit Charlie or respond to his aggression with violence.

One evening in the second week of January, I took my writing up to Mike's so I could work while also squeezing in a bit more time with Charlie. Mike didn't seem to understand the pressure I felt from the work that was upon me, or my single-minded dedication and concern over Charlie. "You get to write a book, that's what you've wanted to do," he said. But the task, especially in the time frame I agreed to, was far from the romantic idea of an artist lounging about with pen in hand. And repairing things with Charlie was as important as my commitment to my publisher; his well-being was my responsibility. After brief hellos to Mike and Mark, I went upstairs with my laptop and my papers to work on the bed. Charlie trotted up the stairs with me and curled up next to me as I tried to type. But the TV was on in the living room, and Mike and Mark were downstairs talking about slaughtering pigs, and the noise floated up to the second story and I couldn't concentrate, couldn't get lodged in any stream of thought. I lay on the bed and stroked Charlie's curled body, kissed his forehead. And I though I didn't want to leave Charlie, I had to work; I would need every minute of the next six months to get the book finished in time. I packed up my bag and slipped out the door. Eli was waiting for me at the cabin with frost coating his whiskers.

I stoked up the fire and put my disappointment aside and worked while Eli slept mashed flat under the woodstove. The night was fifteen degrees below; the thermometer hadn't crested zero in weeks. I was cold all the time and there was nothing to be done about it; there was no point in complaining, it had just become part of life. During my hikes with Charlie with the icy air burning my face, I realized why men, traditionally, had the outdoor roles—it was because they could grow beards. My back and shoulder muscles seized up from being hunched and tense from the cold and I was losing weight; even though I was eating all day long, nothing was sticking to me. I caught my reflection in the glass door at Mike's and I looked like a caricature drawing, long stick legs growing cartoonishly out of my snow boots.

Mike was in a low mood the next evening when we went to feed, disillusioned with his job. "Everyone's flying just to kill a bunch of coyotes and it doesn't even make logical sense," he said as we drove to put gas in the truck. "It's a waste of airplane fuel to fly between November and February—if you kill 'em out of a lambing area now, it just creates a void that's immediately filled. The coyotes are all running around and pairing up, and if you wait until they establish territory and get ready to have pups, you can take care of the ones you need to, to protect stock. Right now, it's just flying around murdering coyotes, wasting gas." I shook my head and sighed, and caught the new readerboard message out the window. *Blessings of Choice.*

"They've gotten way off track from the original goal of protecting livestock," Mike vented. "It's become based solely on numbers—and not the number of live lambs, but the number of dead coyotes."

We pulled up to the haystack. The bales were frozen together and Mike cursed the ice, and continued to mutter over the politics of his job, oblivious to the breathtaking sunset, deaf to my jokes and puns as I tried to lighten his mood.

The next evening after a full day of work, I scooped up Eli and took him with me up to Mike's. He and Charlie had not seen each other in over a week. When we walked in, Mike was lying on the couch on his stomach, watching Charlie play with a pingpong ball, a small, private smile on his face. Charlie dashed to the door when he saw Eli, craning his neck to get his snout under Eli's chin and lick his face, and then together they took off up the stairs. I joined them on Mike's bed where they were roughhousing, and sat back against the headboard, away from the action, studying Eli. I watched his posture, his body language, took mental notes on how he interacted with Charlie. Eli was calm and fearless with the rambunctious coyote, and Charlie, though he could have killed Eli in a matter of seconds, never once challenged the cat's swats or brush-offs. They sparred playfully and rolled around on the bed, and Eli always won.

I went downstairs and found Mike and Mark in the kitchen, dipping into a tub of strawberry ice cream. Mark scooped a bowl for me, and the clatter of spoons and dishes drew Charlie downstairs to see what was being eaten and if he could have a little. I sat on a bar stool, eating my ice cream in front of Charlie as he sat before me, and then offered him a spoonful. He stood to eat it, but I drew away the spoon and asked him to sit again, and to stay seated while he ate. Several times we repeated this, the continued "sit" while he ate off the spoon. I took a tip from one of the coyote-women and when Charlie did not immediately obey, I ate the waiting spoon of ice cream myself.

The next morning, I walked up after an early morning of work to take Charlie on a walk. We started out on the BLM road and then cut down a slope through the sagebrush to the bottom of a massive draw. I kept Charlie at my side, asking him to follow my lead. If he deviated from my path, his leash tangled around one of the many sagebrush that dotted the hillside, and I waited with the leash taut as he turned back around and came to me.

At the bottom of the draw, the narrow trail led us in gentle curves. The once-red walls, now covered in snow, rose at either side, creating a path so private and wonderful, tucked away from the rest of the world. Tiny snowflakes drifted down as we made our way to a frozen stream where sagebrush grew five feet tall along its edge. The ice was a translucent milky-green, and I could see the hoofprints of deer in the ice, frozen into heart-shaped indentations from where they had crossed while the ice was still slush. I walked carefully down the center of the stream on patches of snow as Charlie dashed around, slipping and sliding until he figured out how to walk securely on the ice.

We found ourselves at the BLM fence line below Mike's house and could have easily ducked through the fence and walked the hill up to the house but instead, I turned Charlie around and had him follow our exact trail from where we had come. I could monitor his accuracy for I could see our tracks in the snow. When Charlie veered from the trail of our footprints, I said, *"Hey,"* and stopped moving forward myself, and it did not take long for him to grasp the concept of the challenge. Sometimes, Charlie stopped to sniff a rabbit track that crossed our path, but after a glance in the direction the rabbit had gone, he faced straight ahead and continued to follow our winding tracks. He was more exhausted than I by the time we got back to Mike's.

My walks with Charlie had once again become a respite in my hectic schedule. The following day, I went up to Mike's once he and Mark were gone, had another great walk along the BLM trail with Charlie. We re-

turned just as a blizzard began to blow in and slipped in to Mike's house out of the weather. Charlie curled up on the bed, sleeping cozily; I lay next to him working for a wonderful, peaceful hour. Then Mike came home, angry and tense. He turned on the TV, Charlie woke and leapt off the bed, and I left. I had to take my moments with Charlie when I could, and appreciate those moments and the safety he had up at Mike's.

Later that night I returned to spend some time with Charlie. He was still outside in the yard when I got there, though it was dark. Frost coated his fur, each individual hair. Even at night, the snow glittered from the moonlight. After a pet and a nuzzle, Charlie and I played in the night-light, running circles and romping in the snow. After a while, I sat on my heels in front of him and we just looked into each other's eyes, just caring for each other; it was pure and deep and simple. Charlie reached his snout toward my face and tilted his head up slightly to press his nose, so cold and small, against mine.

I was traveling back and forth between the cabin and Mike's house several times a day to work with Charlie and hike with him, to take photos, and then returning to the cabin to take care of everything I had to do for the blog, the book, and the daily pictures. I tried to take my writing up to Mike's in order to work while being near Charlie, but I had to time it while the house was empty. In fact, I was trying to spend most of my time with Charlie while Mike was away, because I had noticed Charlie's attitude drastically changed toward me when Mike showed up. It wasn't every time, wasn't consistent enough for me to put my finger on the reason or the cause, but often, even when Charlie and I had been easy and playful together for an hour or two, Charlie got visibly tense and snappy when Mike returned to his house. After three weeks, I was at the end of my rope. I had been up and down between the house and the cabin eight times in one day—I simply couldn't figure out where to be. I'd work at the cabin, then go up to be with Charlie, but not feel right at Mike's house and go back down to the cabin, then feel guilty and go back up only to find Charlie napping and head back to the cabin. It was a torment.

When Mike got in, I told him I was considering moving back into my old rental and taking Charlie with me. It was the only way I could think of to work with Charlie and help things improve, and work on the book without having so much time wasted going between the cabin and his house. The other house would provide ample space and safety for Charlie and a discreet yard that opened up from sliding glass doors on the lower level of the house. Charlie would be able to go in and out as he wished, I could work with him steadily throughout the day and still work steadily on the book, and we would be separate from the tense energy that was growing when Mike and I were together. A distancing was occurring between us, and I was no longer picking up the slack during Mike's emotional withdrawals. I felt they stemmed from his refusal to look Tracy's death in the face, and this broke my heart, but I had stopped overcompensating, and started to let go. In moving, I would be able to focus solely on Charlie and my book, and I felt that was what was necessary in order for it to mend.

"You don't even want my help anymore," Mike said, on the defensive.

"It's not that I don't want your help, Mike, it's that there's nothing you can help me with. *I* have to take pictures to send out every day, *I* have to write this book in six months, *I* have to figure out how to get things right between Charlie and me—it's not anything anyone else can do. This isn't about you, Mike, it's about me trying to take care of my responsibilities, and it's not working this way—I can't get a handle on it all."

He turned away.

"Nothing is certain, Mike, I'm just telling you what's running through my head, possible solutions."

Mike left angry and punished me by taking Mark with him to feed the cows. He couldn't have picked a more perfect day, for it was blowing twenty-five miles an hour by the time they fed. Throwing hay off the back of the truck in the wind meant you ended up with your eyes filled with hay dust, and it coated your skin in a wretched, fine, itchy grit. I didn't want to be within fifty feet of a hay bale when it was windy like that.

A few weeks before, Mike had brought up neutering Charlie as a solution, but I didn't want to neuter Charlie in hopes that it would solve a problem if it wasn't the best thing for Charlie. I always felt there was more to the discord than hormones, anyway. But if hormones were creating an internal conflict in Charlie, then I wanted to address that. A few days after the minor blowup with Mike, I spent an evening with Charlie at his house. Charlie and I were alone upstairs, lying side by side in a tender, easy moment. I felt something wash over my mind— that's the only way I can describe it, like a gentle rolling wave that never crests nor breaks—and what was left behind was a knowing that the time was right to neuter him. It was like it was a mind-to-mind transmission from Charlie, and I was so conscious of keeping my own motives aside, I knew it couldn't have come from me.

The next day, I called a professor of animal husbandry whom I had been referred to and had a candid and lengthy conversation about Charlie. I trusted his advice because during the course of our call, he asked great questions. Castrating Charlie was an enormous deal for me personally. In that act, I would be making a permanent commitment to Charlie, and against the backdrop of my past, I took this seriously; I knew the implications. The doctor affirmed everything I had been considering and coming to terms with inside—that Charlie wouldn't last a month in the wild, if not for his own skills then because of hunters, that he was acclimated to humans to such a degree as to be potentially more dangerous than a strictly wild coyote, and that his emotional attachment was proven through his obedience. He believed that neutering was a necessary step to secure Charlie's safety and simply for his own peace of mind, to extinguish conflict inside him.

I did not want to take Charlie to a vet. I knew it would be incredibly stressful on Charlie, and wild animals are much more sensitive to anesthesia. During our call, I asked the doctor if banding Charlie would be a viable form of castration. Banding is commonly used to castrate lambs and calves; it entails stretching a tiny, plump rubber band around the animal's testicles, which cuts off circulation. The testicles dry up and naturally separate from the body and fall off—no surgery, no open wounds—and I believed the day or two of discomfort that would follow the banding would actually be easier on Charlie than a trip to a vet's office. "Absolutely," he said. "I've done it with dogs to great success, and under the circumstances, it would be the best route to take."

Confident from the feeling I had received from Charlie and the conversation with the doctor, I called Mike and relayed all the information and asked if he would be willing to help me the next day. I wanted to do the banding, but I thought I might need Mike's assistance to distract Charlie and keep him somewhat still. "We just have to be calm," I said to Mike, who was all atwitter when I got to his house the next afternoon. "Charlie loves being rubbed on his belly while he's lying on his back—if you can do that, I can slip the band on." Mike agreed but remained tense. We brought Charlie inside and ran upstairs together to play on the bed. I had a metal tool with handles similar to pliers that came to a point where four metal pins sat tightly together, upon which the tiny band was placed. When the handles were squeezed, the pins splayed apart, stretching the band open roughly three inches. I had never banded an animal before, but I had watched Mike band many calves and felt certain I could do it. When Mike had Charlie on his back, I bent over his hind legs with tool in hand, stretched open the band and slipped it over his testicles, and after feeling around with my other hand that all was in order and both balls were trapped, I released the handles and the band tightened up. Charlie was unfazed, but within an hour, the effects took hold. Charlie lay on the bed and didn't move, and the one time he got down to eat, he threw up. While Mike and Mark were downstairs, I spent some time with Charlie upstairs. He was curled in a ball and I spooned my body around his. He licked my hand slowly and tenderly, over and over, as he'd never done before, and in that gesture, it was as if he was showing gratitude and understanding. I stroked his face as he reached up to cover my face with his delicate little licks and then bury his head in my chest. It was a night of sweetness I did not expect.

The next day, Charlie was in obvious discomfort. He snapped at anyone and anything that came near him, even Cupcake, who he usually cowered from. I got close enough to see that his testicles were swelled to twice as large as normal, still producing but, due to the rubberband, unable to circulate into his body. He was angry and in pain and wanted to take it out on someone, so aside from bringing him food and water, I left him alone.

On the third day after the banding, I walked up to Mike's in the afternoon to check on Charlie. It was a mild day in the high thirties, and Charlie and I roughhoused in the yard, laughing and spinning and grinning at each other. As we tussled, I swept his legs out from under him so he landed gently on his side, then rolled him on his back and rubbed his belly. He loved it, writhing with his paws folded on his chest and his ears folded on his head. I rubbed his favorite spot with one hand while, with the other, quickly felt his testicles, the band, and the area around it. His testicles were about half the size they had been before the banding, and a quarter of what they were two days earlier when they had been so horribly swollen. The area above the band was normal and there were no signs of inflammation. After a few quick moments, I brought both hands up to his belly as Charlie grinned and wiggled with glee.

Mike pulled up as I was about to walk home. He pulled me into a hug and asked how things were.

"Why don't we bring Charlie with us to load hay?" Mike said. "I'll load hay, and you can bring your camera and take pictures of Charlie, and he can have a little outing."

"That sounds so great," I said, smiling. "I need to make a few phone calls before five and get my camera, so how about I walk down, and you load up Charlie when you're ready and pick me up at the cabin?"

"OK," Mike said. "See you in a bit."

I hopped in Mike's pickup when he pulled up beside the cabin. Charlie stood between us on the seat. Charlie seemed a little weird and jumpy but I passed it off as he hadn't been in a truck for a while and Mike's dogs were running alongside the pickup, barking like maniacs. When we got to the haystack, Charlie hopped out of the truck after me and ran over to play with the dogs. Mike rounded the stack and I heard the heavy thunk of a bale hitting the truck bed. I wrapped Charlie's leash around my hand and pulled my camera off from around my neck. Charlie scampered up to my knees and then ran back to the dogs, then turned, ran toward me again, but this time, leapt in the air and clamped down hard on my forearm. He dropped to his hind legs without letting go of my arm and stood there, staring me in the eyes, growling through his jaws, biting my forearm as hard as he could. Flashing through my mind simultaneously was the shock of Charlie's eyes, cold in mine; the excruciating pain all the way to my bones, between the bones of my arm; the fear of him lurching up higher toward my chest or neck or face; and the directives of everything I had been told and read: don't run, don't fight back. And so I just stood there, dumb, and when I realized Charlie wasn't going to stop and this wasn't going to suddenly disappear, I called out for Mike. He was behind the haystack and I screamed louder, "MIKE!" He jogged around the corner of the stack and when he saw Charlie hanging from my arm he dashed over, grabbed Charlie by the collar and pulled him off, took the leash from my hand and tied Charlie, who continued to snarl and snap in my direction, to a fence post. I walked behind the haystack and leaned against it, sobbing, clutching my arm.

Mike came over. "Are you okay?" he asked.

Tears streamed down my face. I nodded, and turned to hide my face. I was wearing the deerskin and Charlie hadn't punctured my skin, but my arm burned with pain and as Mike pulled up my sleeve, I saw there were dents in my arm from Charlie's teeth and they soon grew into small hard bumps like mosquito bites. But the worst pain was deeper inside; knowing the process of trust with Charlie and of confidence in my own self had to start all over again. We had been doing so well, we were on such a roll, and now that momentum was broken.

"It's not you," Mike kept repeating.

"Yes," I sobbed, "it is, or he wouldn't have done it." I couldn't stop crying.

"It's not you, Shreve," Mike said seriously.

I looked at him. "Why are you saying that? What do you mean?"

"Charlie was balking when I took him over to the truck, he didn't want to go, but . . ." Mike trailed off. "But I wanted to score points with you and have a perfect afternoon with the three of us, so I grabbed him and threw him in the truck. That's what this is from. It's not you."

I shook my head. Charlie had been forced to be there, and he took out his frustration on me; he took it out on me because he knew I was the only one he could take it out on.

Mike felt awful and I told him not to beat himself up over it, but later that night, I hit the anger stage about it. I hadn't done anything, and yet I was the one who had to deal with the aftermath. Mike compromised what was dearest to me with the hopes of getting what he wanted, and willingly endangered both Charlie and me. I would never have forced Charlie into the truck; I would never have gone with them if I had known Charlie had been stressed and provoked that way. Now I was back at the beginning. Now our walks, the one part of my day that was a time of peace and joy and connection, was taken away from me and would be a source of stress and worry too, because of Mike.

I spent one day away from Charlie to allow the intense fear to leave my system, and the day after that, I walked up while Mike was at work to take Charlie on a walk. It was the kind of light snowy day that I loved the most—the sky blank and bright white, and tiny dry flakes drifted down through the air. Charlie was sitting like a sphinx in the yard when I arrived. I was wearing the deer skin and I carried a deer antler with me. Deer and elk naturally shed their antlers each year and grow new ones, and Mike and I had found many such antlers. I chose a mule deer antler that was comfortable in my hand but fairly large. It had three long tines, two of which formed a neat V. The fork in the antler would serve as a handy and secure way to keep Charlie at bay should he try to attack me; the pressure of his chest or neck in the crook of the V would allow me to guide him away, and the softly rounded nature of the antler itself would not hurt Charlie if I had to use it to push him back. I was nervous, but made myself try to overcome it. We walked the BLM trail, never veering from it. Charlie was pleasant and happy, and I was successful against my fear about 70 percent of the time.

That night, I called my former landlady and asked her about moving back into the house, which I knew was unoccupied. She was stunned. The night before she had been at a party in Boulder, Colorado, and everyone was talking about The Daily Coyote. She was sympathetic to the situation and entranced by Charlie, and because I felt this move was my only hope for success with Charlie, I offered to pay her in rent the equivalent of her mortgage so we could move in immediately. I was making that very amount from the website.

Eleven

February

The first week of February, I moved over to the new house alone. Eli had left the cabin at four that morning and I knew he'd be gone for hours. I didn't want to wait for him and I needed to get settled into the house myself before bringing Charlie over. There was heartache in moving. I adored the cabin, and knew I always would; but as a snake sheds its skin in order to grow, I had to leave the space that had contained me. I stripped the bed, unplugged my computer, loaded my truck, and left. Alone in the new house, I kept myself busy and my mind occupied by Charlie-proofing the main rooms, moving the owner's books off all but the highest shelves, and putting her keepsakes—dolls, dream catchers, and baskets—in the master bedroom, a room I never used and which door could stay permanently closed. I had brought Charlie's toys from the cabin and arranged them on the lower shelves of the bookcase, set up my office downstairs, washed my sheets and made up the bed in the smaller up-stairs bedroom, and crashed. When I woke in the morning, I wandered out into the kitchen and realized I only needed to boil enough water for coffee, for there was a sink down the hall where I could brush my teeth and wash my face with warm running water.

I was in a quandary about how to get Charlie from Mike's house to the new house. I would normally have had Charlie jump in my truck and drive over, but after his last experience in a truck, I worried that Charlie would resist getting in or get violent about it. We had gone on several good walks since Charlie had attacked my arm, but the incident was still too recent for me to feel completely confident. If we walked, though it was only about a quarter of a mile, we would have to be on the county road for much of it and then weave through the subdivision, passing several strange houses and horses. I didn't know how stressful that would be for Charlie, and having him go after me in a moment of stress in the middle of the subdivision would be very bad coyote PR. After weighing the options and the variables within each, I determined that driving would be the quickest and the least stressful for both of us, if Charlie would get in the truck. Would he even do it? Would it be safe for *me* in the truck?

At around ten a.m. I headed over, knowing Mike was working and would be gone for much of the day. I stopped at the cabin on my way up to Mike's and called Eli multiple times, but he wasn't there. I had hoped Eli would show Charlie by his example that the truck and the new house were nothing to be afraid of, but as Eli was not to be found, I was on my own. Charlie was lounging in the yard when I got there. I went inside and cut a sausage into very small pieces, stuck them in a baggie, and with my lures in hand, led Charlie into the driveway. When we got near the truck, Charlie ran the opposite direction, afraid, his body low. I held tightly to his leash so that he ran out of rope and had to stop about twenty feet from the truck. Calmly, I opened the passenger door and sat on the running board, and tossed a bit of sausage to Charlie so it landed about two feet from him. Charlie edged toward the sausage with his eyes on the truck and ate it quickly; as he did, I wound up the slack in the leash so he was now two feet closer. I cooed to Charlie and sang to him; he walked a semicircle at the end of his line but every once in a while, took a step closer on his own. I tossed him bits of sausage at intervals, luring him closer. Eventually, Charlie stood just three feet from the open door of the truck. I made sure he was watching me, and placed a slice of sausage on the running board and another on the seat itself. Then I tossed a piece to him, just four inches from him, and as he was eating it, immediately tossed him another, this one halfway between him and the truck. Charlie flickered in a moment of hesitation, then scooped up the second piece of sausage in his mouth and bounded into the open truck and onto the seat, and sat down, looking straight ahead. It took an hour, all told, but in the end it was Charlie who hopped in the truck of his own accord. I wrapped his leash around the back of the passenger seat twice, so that he had room to move around on his side but couldn't get over to my side, jumped in the driver's seat, and away we went.

It was a short drive and I sang to him the whole way. When we pulled up in front of our new home, I unwound the leash and let Charlie out with prayers for a calm integration. Charlie hit the ground in a trot, and with his nose to the ground, canvassed the yard and the trees with curiosity, his manner relaxed. After about half an hour outside, I opened the sliding door into the house and let Charlie off his leash to explore. Charlie sniffed every corner of the lower level, dashed up the stairs, and made two quick rounds of the upper floor. I led him into the bathroom and tapped on the bathtub. Charlie hopped in, turned a circle, and squatted to pee down the drain. Though he would be going outside much of the time, I wanted him to learn immediately that, if he had to go during the night, this was the proper place to pee. Charlie found his toys in the bookcase, selected an old leather strap to chew on, and curled up on the living room carpet in the warmth of the window light, gnawing contentedly.

Our first few days in the house were peaceful and easy; I was thrilled to be back with Charlie, for the simplicity and togetherness that returned immediately. The enormity of the house, which had seemed overwhelming when I had first rented it, was now a great blessing. Charlie spent nights inside, sleeping in the living room, while I slept in the bedroom down the hall with the door closed. There was plenty of room for Charlie to explore, room for me to chase him around the living room. The south wall of the living room was lined with floor-to-ceiling windows where Charlie could curl up in the sun and watch birds or snowflakes out the window.

A pasture, lined with a rail fence, separated the house from the county road. Though other houses stood nearby, the yard was situated between the house and the great pasture, keeping Charlie out of sight. With his long leash tied to the trunk of a tree in the yard, Charlie had range of the yard and could walk up to the sliding glass door and paw at it when he wanted to come in. Though I still loathed his being tethered, this was the best situation we had ever had. He had shade, grass, dirt, and trees; we could see each other through the wall of windows; I could take breaks often to play with him right in the yard and he could come in as he chose.

Mike called, devastated by the move, by the rift between us. "I don't want to keep you and Charlie apart forever." I said, "But Charlie and I have to get back on track and he picks up on the tension between us and it creates tension in him. It just needs to be this way for a while, for everybody's sake."

"No, don't worry about that," Mike said, "he's better off with you, you've given him everything. I just don't know what to do without you both here . . ." He trailed off.

"Mike, you weren't happy before—even when I loved you so completely, you weren't happy. I want you to find your happiness more than anything, but it seems like it always goes back to your guilt, to Tracy. I want you to be able to find *her*."

"I know," he said. "But there's nothing there. Nothing physical. I can't do it if nothing exists."

"She *does* exist. What if her spirit or soul had some choice in the matter? What if it wasn't your fault? She is one of the lucky ones, Mike. At twelve, she got to experience the sun and the snow and horseback rides through the wilderness with you, but she never had to deal with relationships, or worry about money. She got all of the good of this world, and none of the bad."

I went outside with Charlie later that evening. The stars looked different to me than they had at the cabin. I wondered if stars looked different when you were alone.

The next day, Charlie and I ventured out on a hike; we had new property and new areas of BLM to explore. East of the pasture, the land dipped sharply down a steep draw and opened up into untamed red hills dotted with sagebrush and cut with canyons and draws. When we returned to the house, Charlie played outside while I worked. I looked out and saw him sitting in the yard, looking out over the pasture with his back to me, so calm and dear, the tones and pattern of his coat blending in with the dry winter grass around him. I went outside and sat next to him and scratched his head between his ears. His fur was so warm. His eyes closed slightly in the sunlight, his tiny eyelashes honey-colored and tipped with black. We sat, content and connected as I continued to scratch his head. Charlie started to nod off, still seated, but drooping slightly and falling asleep under my hand until he finally lay down in the grass for a nap. I took the opportunity to reach under his tail and feel his testicles. They were still fully attached to his body but the mass was hard and flat, like a dried apricot. When Charlie woke a few hours later, he scratched at the door to come in and we made cookies in the kitchen together. He stood beside me the whole time; I gave him the eggshells and we both tasted the batter. Then we lay in the sun-drenched living room together, spooning on the floor. I couldn't believe it was so perfect.

By the third day, Eli was still at large. I had been making twice daily trips to the cabin in the morning and evening in hopes of finding him, of timing my arrival perfectly with his return or finding him curled up in the window box, waiting. I began to worry that I would never find him; that he would think I had abandoned the cabin and moved on without him, that he would permanently join the band of feral cats he cavorted with all night, or that he would try to find me at Mike's house and get eaten by his dogs. On the third luckless day, I stuck a short piece of kindling between the door and the jamb to keep it propped open a few inches, filled his dish with food, and threw an old sheet on the bed in hopes he would enter and stay put long enough for me to come back and get him. On the fifth day, I stopped by the cabin on my way home from the post office and found Eli curled up in the loft. I scooped him up, showered him with kisses, and drove to our new home with Eli on my lap.

Charlie and Eli had not seen each other in almost a month, and I didn't know exactly how the reunion would go. I was certain they would remember each other, but I wasn't sure how Charlie would treat Eli–if he would be as submissive as he always had been. With Charlie outside, I carried Eli into the house via the kitchen door, on the opposite side of the house from the yard, and once the cat had reacquainted himself with the house where he had spent his kittenhood, I let Charlie in. Charlie dashed up the stairs and into the living room with his tail wagging like a plane's propeller. His ears were flattened against his head as he wiggled his way toward Eli and somersaulted onto the ground in front of the cat, lying on his back with his paws curled on his chest, reaching up to cover Eli's face in coyote licks. Eli stood for Charlie but made no obvious show of emotion, but that was Eli's way.

At the end of the first week in the house, Charlie and I headed out on our morning walk. Though snow covered the ground, the sun was out and the sky a perfectly uniform periwinkle blue. We wandered along the bottom of the steep draw that curved beneath the pasture toward the road but was protected from sight and sound by steep walls and sagebrush that grew as tall as I was. We hiked up a finger of a draw and I jumped slightly when I saw that a dead deer lay before us, a large buck without his antlers–they had either just dropped, as deer antlers naturally do in late winter, or were about to and had been pulled off. The buck had a perfectly round bullet hole in his side, likely poached by a neighbor who wanted the deer out of his haystack. It had not been dead long; its eyes were sunken, but that happens soon after death, and there was no sign of animals or bugs having yet discovered the carcass. I kept Charlie just out of reach of the deer, knowing if he got his teeth into it we would be there all day. When we returned home, I tied Charlie in the yard and looked around in the garage until I found a hacksaw, and walked back out to the deer. With a firm grip on the top front leg, I began sawing it off at the joint. It was difficult work, sawing through the bone, and I pushed the saw through the deer's leg rhythmically, working up a light sweat. After I had sawed about halfway through, I used my feet as a brace against the deer's upper leg and wrenched the lower leg back toward me to break the bones. I sawed through the remaining tendons and hide and I had a foreleg to take back for Charlie. Charlie watched me cross the pasture back to him, and began dancing in circles as I approached with the deer leg in my hand. "Sit," I asked Charlie, and he wiggled into a sit. The moment I offered him the leg he snatched it with delight and was off bounding around the yard with the leg in his mouth, tossing his head and prancing. I went inside to work on the book, happy that whenever I glanced out the window I saw him sitting in the winter sun, chewing on the deer leg held between his paws.

Midday, Charlie came inside to nap in the sunny window. I was working on the sofa on my laptop, and smiled to myself at his sweet posture. He lay on his side, his body a little hunched at the spine, and his tail curved down along the back of his legs. His four legs were perfectly straight and his feet all met in one point, like he could be calf-tied. His neck was stretched out on the floor, curving up and back so that he rested on his chin with his nose pointing behind him.

The phone rang and Charlie woke with a start, and jumped to his feet when I got up. His eyes were cold, staring into mine, and he advanced toward me, growling with his lips pulled up to reveal his teeth. I backed up a few steps and slipped out the kitchen door, leaving Charlie in the house. "Call you back," I blurted, left the phone on the outside steps. I walked with an accelerated heartbeat around the house to the sliding door, where Charlie came down to meet me face-to-face on the other side of the glass. I opened the door just enough to slip my hand in and clip on Charlie's leash, then, leaving the sliding door open just an inch or so, went into the garage. The door between the house and the

garage was situated so that I could stand in the garage behind the door and stretch my arm through the doorway to push open the sliding glass door just enough for Charlie to squeeze out. Once he was in the yard, I stepped into the house. As I slid the door closed between us, he looked at me, cocked his head, and whimpered, as if to say, *Why don't you come play with me out here?* I was so perplexed. How could he go from being a sweetheart all day, to growling severely at me, to being a sweetheart minutes later? I left him outside and worked for a while, then joined him and chased him around the yard at dusk, laughing out loud, Charlie grinning with his tongue flapping the whole time. We went inside together and I fed Charlie, let Eli out for his nightly prowl, and Charlie curled up in the living room when I went to bed.

Eli meowed at the door at five in the morning. I cursed the hour, threw on a sweatshirt, and emerged from the bedroom to let Eli in. I stopped in my tracks, confronted by Charlie, who stood at the end of the hallway with his head low, growling, staring straight at me. He took a slow, deliberate step forward, and then another, growling louder, his eyes never leaving mine. I whipped back into my bedroom and shut the door. My heart was racing. Eli was still meowing relentlessly outside and I could hear Charlie growling as he pawed at my door. I stood there, and I wanted to call Mike. I knew he would drive over in a heartbeat and get Charlie on his leash outside, but I knew bringing him into the equation would complicate things, and I also knew I couldn't lean on him. I pulled on a pair of jeans, put my hair back in a ponytail, and grabbed the wooden armchair that sat in the corner of the bedroom. I opened the door, and clutching the arms of the chair with the feet out toward Charlie, used it to push him away from me down the hallway. This sent Charlie into a rage. His teeth were fully bared and he began psychotically attacking one of the legs of the chair, becoming a snarling wood chipper before my eyes. He did not want to allow me in the living room, and his ferocity was numbing.

I got myself to the kitchen door and opened it to let Eli in. Charlie's demeanor changed in an instant and he was nothing but wags and kisses for the cat. I backed myself out the door, walked around the house barefoot in the dark, and with the technique I had used the day before, got Charlie's leash on him and got him outside without us ever coming into direct contact. I went back to bed for an hour and a half, and when I got up and warily checked on Charlie, standing inside but with the sliding door partially open, he ran up to me with his ears folded on his head, full of sweetness and affection.

I took him for a morning walk through the BLM, but first dug out the old deer antler and carried it with me, just in case. The morning was gorgeous with the first feeling of Spring's warmth in the air. Charlie was perfectly obedient. He came when I asked, leaving his route and scent trails to follow me. We found patches of untouched snow lying in drifts on the north sides of the draws, deep and white, and Charlie plowed through snow up to his shoulders. We laughed and ran and both fell a few times, but even that was fun, the snow soft and welcome in the light, balmy morning. Yet even in light of such companionship, I decided that from that point on, Charlie would sleep outside at night.

A few simple, easy days passed, marked by hikes with Charlie deep into the BLM under gorgeous blue skies and afternoons spent in the living room, writing while Charlie napped at my feet. After playing together in the house in the late evening, I let Charlie outside and he sat in the yard overlooking the pasture, watching the night happenings that were invisible to me. At dawn, I'd find him fluffed in a ball under one of the trees, and let him in while I made coffee and got the morning's work done before our daily walk. When we returned from a great hike through the BLM, Charlie came inside for his midday nap. I was ready to lie down myself, with my notes and my laptop, to work on the book on the floor in the sun. Charlie aimlessly circled the living room, looking for the right spot to curl up in, and as I gathered my work, I got a quick hit of feeling that I should wait until after Charlie lay down to lie down myself. I dismissed the thought; I wanted to get started, so I propped up pillows to support my neck and lay back, my knees bent, the laptop resting against my thighs. Charlie walked over to me, walked the length of my body, and put his chin over my right knee and began to growl. It was a physical demonstration of dominance, of being over me. I lay still as stone but his growling became deeper and more intense. With a slight flick of my wrist, I tossed my pen, hoping Charlie would go after it, but he didn't. I had to get him away from me before I could move. I knew from his growls and from his posture, his raised tail and ears cupped to the front, that if I moved to get up, Charlie would see it as a gesture of confrontation, as instigating a fight, and set into me on the attack. Charlie slowly moved up along my body. My heart was racing and pinpricks of sweat burned from my pores. He reached my head, still rumbling with growls, and sniffed my face, his nose against my skin, my forehead, my neck. He pawed my scalp, standing over me. I was terrified. I meowed. "Kitten!" I exclaimed, in the high voice I always greeted Eli with. "Hi, Kitten!" Charlie bounded off of me and ran to the kitchen door, his tail wagging in excitement, looking for the phantom cat. I leapt to my feet and grabbed the deer antler which I had left on the kitchen table after our walk two days earlier. But by then, Charlie had forgotten all about me; all he cared about was finding Eli, and I easily got his leash on him and let him out into the yard.

I walked back upstairs and burst into tears. Tears of pent-up fear, of frustration, of confusion. I curled into a ball on the floor and cried in heartbreak and anger. Why was this happening? Why was he acting this way with me? I wanted him back, back like it had been in the summertime. I didn't want to fail; I didn't want to fail him. I left him outside for the rest of the day, and in the evening, hoarse and dehydrated from a day of crying, I went out onto the narrow second-story deck above the yard.

Charlie sat in the grass below me, looking up with a message in his eyes, *Come play with me, Shreve*. But I stayed where I was and wept, because I was too scared. Then Charlie put on a show for me with his deer leg, tossing it in the air and twirling it like a baton and leaping in coyote acrobatics. He succeeded in making me laugh, but that just made me even sadder.

That night, it dawned on me that acting—versus reacting—was essential. I was getting attuned enough to Charlie's subtle signs to recognize what emotions he held at any given moment and predict the actions that would come next; I had learned to read the position of his ears, his tail, even his whiskers. And my own intuition was working, if I just listened to it. I needed to start anticipating Charlie, and then redirect him or reposition myself so that a given situation never had the chance to escalate. But that was only an interim measure. The bigger issue, I still had to fix: it was not about Charlie biting or attacking me, it was about him believing that he *could* bite me, that he was allowed to bite me. This was what I had to change.

For my own safety, I had to set parameters. Parameters were necessary as a demonstration of my dominance, as guidance for Charlie, and also as a reality check for me. That day had been a close call, and I couldn't let myself be so vulnerable. My free and easy love was no longer appropriate, and violent discipline was never an option for me. Structure, though it went against my very grain, was my only hope.

The next day I woke up nervous, lay in bed, thought about the task ahead. I told myself I could lie there and bemoan the state my life was in, or I could start moving, doing, and living to change it. I took the notepad from my nightstand and wrote the words "Parameters. House Rules. Rhythmic Measure." I was not sure of the ways I would implement these things, but kept the themes in my mind as I began the day.

While the water on the stove boiled for coffee, I located the antler from where I had left it the day before, and vowed to have it with me at all times when Charlie and I were together. We set out on an early walk and I kept the antler tucked under my arm, but never once had to actively use it as we traversed the land behind the house, running down the narrow trails the deer had stamped out across the rolling red hills. When we got back to the house, I left Charlie outside even though he wanted to come in. I stroked his face from the doorway, then went inside and made elk stew. Once everything was in the pot and simmering, I went outside with small bits of elk meat and asked Charlie to sit and stay numerous times for the elk, and then let him in but kept the antler close. He curled up to nap in the living room while I went downstairs to work on the computer, setting the antler on the floor beside my desk as I did. At one point, I went upstairs to get a file and Charlie stood at the sound of my feet on the stairs. I had the antler in my right hand and crested the stairs. He didn't growl; instead, he plopped back down and rolled onto his back as an invitation for me to rub his belly. I did; his eyes half opened in animal ecstasy, and I leaned down to kiss his muzzle, kiss between his ears.

The tender moment notwithstanding, my fear was an issue. I couldn't believe how afraid I was, how much fear I now had around Charlie. I noticed that I often backed away from him, even if it was only minutely, or only in my shoulders. I was doing it, and it gave Charlie more power—I knew how my confidence was strengthened when Charlie backed away from me or rolled onto his back. Throughout the recent difficulties, our walks had consistently been the only time when Charlie and I were totally comfortable together. Charlie never challenged me on our walks, they were a time of simple joy and togetherness, when we were happy and worked together. So, to increase this time, this way of being together, I increased our walks to three a day.

I sat down at the kitchen table and wrote out a daily schedule for us to keep, down to the hour:

Eli meowed at the door between 4 and 5; I let him in and went back to bed.

I got up at 6 and let Charlie in, made coffee, and did the morning's internet work while Charlie made the rounds of the house and played with Eli. If he growled at me, I would immediately take him back outside. If he was pleasant, I roughhoused with him, chased him around the coffee table, and rubbed his body.

At 7, we went out for our first walk, until 8:30.

When we returned, Charlie got an egg in a dish outside and I made sure he had fresh water; he stayed outside while I worked for half an hour.

At 9, I let him come inside to be social with Eli and me.

At 9:30, Charlie and Eli went outside together.

At 11, they both came in for naps. Eli took the dog bed and Charlie got the floor.

At 1, Charlie went outside.

From 1:30 to 2:30, we had our second hike.

From 2:30 to 3, he played outside.

From 3 to 5, he was in again, for another rest.

From 5 to 6, we went on an evening walk around the pasture.

From 6 to 7, he was outside.

At 7, he came in for dinner and playtime.

At 9, he went out for the night.

On our walks, Charlie and I left and came back via the same route every day for rhythm and consistency, then took different trails once we were in the BLM for variation, stimulation, and discovery. Charlie had to exit and enter the pasture by going through the gate, not under the fence. If he ducked under the fence, I stopped and waited for him to crawl back under and then reexit through the gate, which he learned quickly. In addition, Charlie had to sit before coming in, before going out, before getting treats or toys, and before getting his dinner.

I dreaded the schedule. I had never done well with order or consistency; I felt intrinsically repelled by it and did not like it. But it was essential that I learn to do it; not just to learn, but to *do* it, completely; to be consistent and solid and strong. I didn't yet know all the steps it would take to get Charlie and me where we needed to go, but I did know this was the one in front of me. It took great effort, but after a couple of days of trying and failing, I was able to stick to the schedule precisely. Charlie and I hiked for a total of five hours that day, and I was excited and hopeful about the plan.

The following day, I slept hard and didn't wake until seven, probably due to the five hours of exercise the day before, but to keep to the schedule, Charlie and I went straight out on a walk, before I had coffee or sent out the The Daily Coyote photos. The sun was just coming up, rising above the snow-covered buttes. It was a pleasant, silent walk; Charlie and I were very much inside ourselves but connecting even so. I stopped, at one point, and pet him, and Charlie leaned against my knees, relaxing into me, looking up into my eyes.

On our way back to the house, we found a rib cage of a deer that wasn't yet fully bleached; it still had a bit of stuff left on the bones. It was frozen to the ground. I broke off two ribs to take home for Charlie, and as I did so, a little shard of bone flew off. Charlie grabbed it and trotted home with it sticking sideways out of his mouth like a cigar.

During his time alone outside, he lay in a patch of grass, gnawing on his ribs with dedication.

On our midday walk, Charlie and I hiked straight up and down the canyons and draws. It was hard work and felt good. Patches of snow were melting in the sun, turning the red dirt into gooey mud for the day was warm and I was stripped down to a t-shirt. That evening we canvassed the pasture, exploring every corner, Charlie sniffing every rock and shrub. He sped out from me like a rocket, his body flattening and seeming to stretch out into a line as he streaked across the pasture and then back to me, and I thought how perfect it would be to fence in such a space for Charlie. But first the ground had to thaw.

That night was a lunar eclipse. As the shadow of the earth crept across the moon, I went outside to sit and watch with Charlie. The moon was red, and as the eclipse became total, a shooting star streaked through the sky beside it. I finally went to bed at eleven-thirty and awoke all too soon to Eli meowing at the door at four-thirty the next morning. When I let him in, I saw by the full moon that Charlie had wrapped the full length of his line around a tree. Knowing I couldn't sleep with Charlie bound in such a way, I got dressed and when I went outside, I saw by the bright moonlight that he had not only wrapped himself around the tree, but had gone over and under the rope in an attempt to unwind himself, so it was twisted as well. Charlie was on the defensive, most likely because he was stuck at the base of the tree, but I had my antler with me and made a game out of unwinding him, talking the whole time, giving Charlie a verbal play-by-play of what we were doing. "Go around," I said, as I lured him around the tree in one direction. "Now under," and held the rope high so he could duck under it to untwist it. "Now over it . . . now back around the other way," and Charlie pranced around and around the tree like a pony on a lead.

We went inside and Charlie and Eli made me laugh as they played together, Eli lying on his back on the kitchen floor swatting at Charlie, and Charlie turning around in tight circles, licking the cat every chance he could get. Charlie sprawled out under my computer desk while I took care of the morning's work, and at seven we went out for the first of our three hikes.

My body was becoming a machine, solid and efficient muscle that took me anywhere afoot. A lone deer stood at the horizon on a ridge of red wall, silhouetted against the sunrise. Charlie and I were beginning to move as a unit. I had had a restless night, stressed about the debates that still raged in the reader-comments section of the website, the book deadline, and thoughts of Mike. But I was able to let go of all of it, and nothing existed but the land, the hint of warmth in the air, the great sky, my body moving, and Charlie there beside me.

When Charlie came in later that morning to nap in the sunny window light, I lay beside him to investigate the progress of the banding. Though his scrotum was still very much attached, the separation had begun, and there was a slight crescent shape of light pink skin where the banded area had separated from Charlie's body gradually enough to allow his body to heal simultaneously and there was no open wound or sore. I dipped a Q-tip in hydrogen peroxide and swabbed the area just to be safe, but even that did not rouse Charlie from sleep.

Charlie hadn't growled at me in several days, but I kept the deer antler with me for my own confidence. Our relationship was improving drastically; I noticed a new kind of communion emerging between us. It was different from the open affection of earlier months, but actually far more satisfying, more conscious. And I was shocked to discover that I was benefiting from the schedule as well. I became much more efficient with my work, knowing I had certain pockets of time to work without distraction, and certain times to let go of my work completely. I was able to focus on the moment, and I was able to really notice how I spent my time.

The comments on the website had slowly gotten out of hand. Though several regulars posted captions and commentaries on the daily photos that gave me daily smiles, there were a growing number of derogatory comments, directed both toward me and other commenters, and actual fights were beginning to break out. When I saw how much time and energy I spent on monitoring the comments, time that was diverted from Charlie and the book, I took the comment option off the site and immediately felt a huge burden disappear. I had been so busy I hadn't left the house in days, and so while Charlie napped inside, I ran to the post office to pick up my accumulated mail. I laughed as I passed the church readerboard. It had one word for me: *"Footprints."*

As Charlie and I got ready for our third walk at sundown, I realized he was no longer jumping up on me in excitement as he usually did when I untied him—he was jumping next to me, and putting his paws on the tree trunk instead. It was a gray evening, windy and cold, but Eli scampered out in a yellow streak and joined us in the pasture. It had been ages since the three of us had gone on a walk together. Charlie was so excited, he was practically running on top of Eli. Eli, in turn, gave a few warning meows and repeatedly tried to duck under Charlie, to no avail. Finally Eli launched himself into the air, level with Charlie's head, and whopped him across the face with his paw. Charlie ran sideways, with Eli hopping along beside him, continuing to box midair until he felt he had made his point. Halfway through our round of the pasture, Eli began to sulk because he didn't like getting his paws wet in the mud, and so I carried him the rest of the way home with Charlie trotting along beside me.

I woke the next morning to a gentle dusting of snow out the windows. The sky was clear, but a cold wind cut across the pasture. I was in the mood to work and did not want to go outside, but took Charlie out at seven for our walk as scheduled. It was cold, but great fun to watch Charlie scamper through the new snow, and as the land lightened, the wind died down and a springish morning bloomed, and I wanted to stay out in the hills with him all day. We ran down the trails together and I marveled at Charlie's grace and agility. Instead of going up and down the narrow draws, we jumped over them, running fast to build speed and leaping over the chasms, and after crossing about fifteen draws in this manner, I realized it was Leap Day, the twenty-ninth of February.

Twelve

March

February in Wyoming always featured a lovely tease of sun-filled days and t-shirt afternoons; then we'd plummet back to winter come March with dreary weather, snow, and the addition of wind. March 1 was a rumbling mix of mild sun, wind, and heavy gray skies, and after a gusty night, I woke on the second to patchy snow on the ground and no stars visible for the clouds.

I let Charlie in and we deviated from our schedule; the wind had come in strong and was blowing twenty-five miles an hour. By eight-thirty, it had calmed down to fifteen, still unpleasant but at least tolerable, and I bundled up in my deerskin and a thin wool hat. Charlie and I wandered through the BLM but kept to the bottom of draws as shelter from wind.

Two weeks earlier, I had sent The Daily Coyote subscribers my story of sawing off the leg of the poached deer, along with photographs of Charlie playing with it in utter delight. I received strong feedback from some people who were disturbed and shaken by the images. I thought long and hard about why, and out in the BLM that gusty day, I realized once again just how wide the chasm is between city and country, and the disparity between urban life and rural. I had been living the transition from one into the other, and like growing out one's hair, I didn't notice the changes until someone from outside remarked on what had become a drastic difference. The emails I had received reminded me how many people in America have no concept of what it's like to be responsible for one's own survival—the basics of food and shelter. I had been one of them. After spending years in New York and San Francisco, I knew what city survival entailed—making money to buy food and pay rent, carrying mace. The basic, physical survival I'd experienced in Wyoming, especially in the cabin, was completely different. No matter how I felt inside, or what the weather was doing outside, I had to chop wood, split kindling, build fires in order to be warm; haul water from outside in order to drink. I had to climb up the roof in a storm to nail down the tin, because otherwise the whole roof could go. I had to learn to plan ahead in order to eat because there were no grocery stores nearby, no takeout or delivery. The world of conveniences fell away, became a fable, when the things I needed to survive I had to rely on myself to do. I still had the luxuries of electricity, of a grocery store to buy food and an internet to order jeans that were delivered to my door. But the things I did have to do gave me perspective, and having to provide the basics for myself made me understand a little of what life is like for the wild animals. Their life is not easy, it is not safe, it is not luxurious or certain. To survive takes extraordinary competence and quite a bit of luck.

We romanticize that wild animals enjoy an idyllic life of freedom, when really, they are fighting to survive, for food and shelter and safety and against the infringements of man. Death serves in nature. The soil is fortified by the bones; animals and birds and bugs live off the carcass. In nature, there is honor in being eaten. To me, the poached deer was beautiful in providing its body to the living animals that were trying to survive. And I believe this works on a human level as well, although it is somewhat taboo in our society. I believe we can learn to use death, and let the gifts of the dead help us to become stronger. Our society responds to death by mourning, and usually, mourning is the stopping place. It is not the stopping place. I believe there is nourishment and strength to be found, if only we were not so afraid of it.

I noticed I hadn't been carrying the antler around for two or three days. It wasn't a conscious decision, and I still carried it with me on our walks, but I found myself getting comfortable around Charlie again. Our interactions had vastly improved, though I sensed that something was still off, something subtle, that I couldn't put my finger on. We were getting closer, but had not yet arrived.

By the end of the first week of March, the sun managed to peek out from behind the gray and the air was deliciously still. Charlie and I celebrated the beautiful day with a long walk deep into the BLM, exploring new and farther banks of red rock and the draws hidden at their base. The day was warm and the hike long enough that I peeled off layers until I was down to my tank top, my arms and shoulders bathed in the sunlight. Charlie and I followed a deer trail home that traversed a high, steep bank, then dropped down to dip and rise along the contours of the draws. Charlie had been following me, but when we reached the first small draw he leapt across as I ran down and back up the other side,

and we landed on the narrow path on the opposite side at the same moment, and I stepped on one of his paws by accident and bad timing.

Charlie yelped and then stared at me, bared his teeth, and lunged for me. I whipped the antler from under my arm, where I had gotten in the habit of carrying it, and positioned it between us, keeping him a foot and a half away from me. As he moved, I moved the antler so that it stayed between us, so that when Charlie tried to get closer, he bumped into the crotch of the tines. I held tightly to his leash with my left hand as Charlie jumped and snarled and tried to get me back for stepping on his foot. After several minutes, sweating in the sun at the base of the great red hill, Charlie backed off. "Go," I said to him, and nodded toward the house. I wanted Charlie to lead the rest of the way, because I did not trust him beside or behind me. Something was still amiss. I was still not the alpha in Charlie's eyes, even though I was technically performing as such, and it was because I was not the alpha in my own eyes.

When we got back home, I called my aunt. In addition to raising both a rottweiler and a pit bull mix that she and her husband had adopted from shelters, she was versed in the metaphysical—emotion, intention, the drives behind the physical body. I needed to talk out what was going on, to understand the bigger picture, and to hopefully glean a greater awareness of the situation through any insight she had to offer. I gave Martha a quick rundown of what had happened, both good and bad, over the past weeks, and the rift in communication that still existed between Charlie and me.

"The task for both of you," Martha said, "is that you each need to surrender. Charlie needs to get to the point where he can surrender to you, because he trusts you, and you need to surrender in a different way, to the reality that life is not always perfect, not for anyone or anything, and you have to allow that part of the process, not only for yourself, but for those around you."

She went on. "Charlie doesn't have to be perfect–like any of us, he can have bad days, but that doesn't have to mean everything; it doesn't have to define everything. And he plays a part in this relationship you're in–his spirit chose to get involved in this life with you, from the very beginning, when he was sitting at the edge of that den as a baby. I believe his spirit chose to enter into a life in between, a life bridging the wild and the domestic. So some of what's going on is going on because it's a lesson for him as well as you."

Her words made sense to me, and they corresponded with the first words Mike had said when he drove up to the cabin with Charlie wrapped in his shirt: *"Something came over me; I can't explain it . . ."* And without releasing myself from responsibility, I could finally see the duality involved, could finally see that we were two parts working together *and* individually. And by releasing myself from the thing in its entirety, letting go of all the guilt I held about the imperfections of Charlie's life, I could finally step into the position I was meant to take, which was also the position Charlie needed me to be fully anchored in and which, ironically, would afford him the peace of mind and peace of being that he had not yet been given the chance to experience in the eleven months of his life.

The light went on inside me. *I have to become the energetic alpha.*

"Energetic alpha" was the only term I could think of to articulate the state of being alpha from the inside out. The epiphany itself caused the result; the epiphany, along with the commitment to live it. Outwardly, I didn't do much differently. I let go of any preconceived ideas I had about living with a coyote and asked myself to be flexible and aware enough to accept Charlie for everything he was. The key was being in control without being controlling.

I stopped walking around him. Instead, if Charlie stood in my path, I walked into him, and after a day and a half, he was moving out of my way. I stopped giving myself up to care for him—which is not to say I stopped providing him with everything he needed. It was an intangible, nearly imperceptible change, one of intention rather than action. Most of all, I stopped feeling guilty, stopped spending every ounce of my energy trying to save Charlie from the fact that his life wasn't perfect. Other shifts came along with this. I let go of my remorse over Mike's unhappiness, of wanting to fix his problems and cure his pain. This seems like such a common female thing, to lose oneself completely when trying to take care of others, but really, it is just another form of control, one that grants no faith in the other person and denies that they have the power and ability to help themselves. It was not my job to save his life; it was his job, and I left his life to him.

Immediately, the dynamics between Charlie and me did a 180. A distinct change had occurred between us—a change in how Charlie related to me. And as the Ides of March approached with doom for the superstitious, Charlie and I were in the middle of a breakthrough. Our bond was tighter than it had ever been when he was young and sleeping on my bed, before any of the problems began. Rather than a human-based emotional connection, it had morphed into an incredibly intense mental connection, one based on communication and respect.

I woke to Charlie howling alongside Eli meowing to come in. I let them in, and when I had coffee in hand, the three of us went outside. I sat in a rusty chair with Eli purring on my lap and Charlie standing calmly beside me, watching the sunrise as I petted his back.

On our morning walk, Charlie and I moved together as if we were joined by more than the leash, our movements in perfect sync. His coloring fascinated me, the way it could change and keep him camouflaged depending on the surroundings and even the light. When we were in the shade, and frost still clung to the ground and accentuated the icy sage, his coat was silver and muted, and he looked frosty himself. Then, when we rounded a bend and hit the sunny side of a ridge, Charlie's coat became a bold pattern of rust and black, mimicking the bright sun on red dirt and hard, black shadows, and white highlights like the glinting sunlight.

We had been finding all sorts of bones and animal parts on our walks, and I decided that instead of stopping midwalk while Charlie chewed on them out in the hills, I would carry the treasures home and give them to Charlie after the walk. Halfway through our spin through the hills, Charlie came upon a section of vertebrae. "Charlie," I said, "I'll bring it home; you can have it at home," and when I reached down to take it from him, he released it. He walked beside me the whole way home and though he obviously wanted the vertebrae and gazed at it often and with longing, he never jumped up or tried to take it from me. I gave it to him in the yard, and he spent the rest of the morning tossing it around, burying it, and unburying it.

Every day now during Charlie's naps on the living room floor, I investigated the status of his castration. All the fur was still attached, as was the tiny green rubberband, but the banded section was slowly and naturally separating from his body. There was a half-moon of pale scar tissue where the separation had already occurred and healed, and at the base, where it still attached, was a thin area of pink skin, like a rug burn; not an open wound and not actively bleeding. Charlie wasn't at all bothered by my fiddling around, but when I swabbed peroxide on the area with a Q-tip, he leapt up and raced around the living room in tight circles with his tail straight out and an expression of *What the heck was that?* After about three lightning-speed rounds, he hunched up his back and scooched along the floor on his butt, his hind feet straight in the air, pulling himself with his front legs. And that must have satis-

fied him, for he curled up again and was ready for a nuzzle on the forehead.

That evening, I got a call from Mike. At the end of our conversation about cows and Charlie and work, he told me he had gone into the basement the night before and looked through all the boxes of Tracy's things, which had been packed up and stacked in a dark corner for the nine years since her death. "It was so hard, I considered a bullet as an answer to the pain," he said, "but all the little things about her that I'd buried came back . . ." He trailed off for a moment. "This might sound really weird," he said when he went on, "but now I see all the ways she was coming to me through you."

I sucked in my breath. "What do you mean?" I asked.

"Well, just little things," he said. "Things that might not mean anything to anyone else, but, like the way you love honey–that girl would eat honey by the spoonful just because she could, and you buy honey a gallon at a time. And the way you look at your horse; I've never seen anyone but Tracy look at a horse like that."

"What else?" I asked.

"Well, I found this deerskin shirt that was hers–I had completely forgotten about it. It was made at the same time as the one I gave you. She never took that thing off, and I don't think you've worn anything but that deerskin for three months, even when you weren't around Charlie. And the cradleboard–you touched it every single time you walked past it. Tracy loved it, she'd throw fits if I ever put Kadi in it, and it was like she was touching it through you, or reminding me of her . . ." His voice was shaky and pained, but reverent. "Now I know I can find Tracy in snowflakes and sunrises. Now I can feel peace."

When we got off the phone, I lay back on the couch, struck by Mike's raw emotion, by his simple honesty, by his courage. And I smiled for them both.

. . .

The ground was beginning to thaw, and the time had finally arrived for me to order a fence. I was thrilled at the prospect of freeing Charlie from his line, and set to work on determining what type of fence would be the best. A coyote can climb an eight-foot chain-link fence, and swiftly dig under it as well, if it is not buried. Chain-link seemed too risky; I wanted a fence that Charlie wouldn't test. After much internet research, I found a company that sold lengths of electrified netting with fiberglass fence posts woven into the net. It was four feet high, and came in lengths of 164 feet that could be joined together indefinitely as long as I reinforced the corners with additional posts. The netting provided security beyond simple electric tape or wire. The height concerned me, for Charlie would be able to clear the four-foot fence in a leap, unless he shied away from the fence altogether.

I began to carefully observe how Charlie investigated the different fences we came upon during our walks. Each time we came to a fence, Charlie sniffed it before proceeding. If it was a barbed-wire or twisted-wire fence, he ducked underneath, and if it was woven wire, he always searched for a place to slip under, and I never once saw him calculate how to jump over, even though he could have cleared a three-and-a-half-foot woven-wire fence with ease. His idiosyncrasy with cactus helped me with my decision as well; after Charlie had stepped on cactus twice and gotten pricked, he still, eight months later, obsessively avoided them, going so far as to find a route to walk around even the smallest clumps rather than jumping over them. My theory, based on these observations, was that if I got an electric fence, Charlie would first investigate it with his nose as he did all other fences, get shocked, and then avoid the fence completely, as he did with cactus.

I decided to fence in all of the lower yard and a section of pasture behind the house, a little over a third of an acre. I measured my stride and paced off the perimeter, then called the company and put in my order without even calculating the total cost. I didn't care what it cost; I finally had the luxury of money in the bank, and Charlie's freedom from his line was more valuable to me than anything else I could have bought.

After placing my order, Charlie and I took a nap together on the floor in the afternoon sun, my body curved along his back, my arm over his body, my face nestled between his giant ears. I couldn't believe how soft the top of his head was; there, it was still as soft as his baby fur had been.

That night, I woke to the screaming wind. It was the sound of war, of violence; it was shaking the house. I looked at my bedside clock. It was only midnight. I got up—I had to check on Charlie—and when I got to the sliding door I saw it was a blizzard outside. The wind shook the trees; snowflakes and dry tumbleweeds whizzed past sideways. Charlie ran up when I slid open the door, and I quickly closed it a few inches so he couldn't get in. He sat dutifully before me. "Oh, Charlie," I sighed. He obviously wanted to come in, and I wanted to let him in. Though I was concerned with what might happen come morning, I decided to try it. "We'll see what happens, Charlie," I said as I let him in. The morning would be a true test to see if the changes of the past two weeks had really taken hold. I spent a few minutes with him in the living room, rubbing him down and watching him play with a stuffed dog with a rattle in its belly. Then I went to my bedroom and closed the door, grabbing the deer antler on the way.

I woke up just before six, before my alarm went off. I got up, acknowledged that I was nervous, and yet curious, about what Charlie's behavior might be like when I left my bedroom and walked out into the living room. I knew I would be able to fight him off with the antler if I had to. I took a few deep breaths, got centered, threw on jeans, a fleece, and socks, and took the deer antler in my hand. I opened the door and slowly walked down the hallway. Charlie was in the same corner of the room where he had stood growling over me a month before. He was curled up, facing the window with his back toward me. He heard me and leaned his neck back to watch as I walked over to him and knelt beside him, at his back. He looked up at me and smiled in recognition, then rolled sideways into my legs to expose his belly for a rub. His body was so warm, his fur thick and dense around my hand and wrist. I saw it had snowed over an inch since midnight, but the wind had quit and the skies were a soft blanket of gray. I made tea and began to write as Charlie woke slowly, then he scratched at the door to go out and explore the new snow. An hour later, it began to snow again. Charlie came in and curled in a ball at the window, his head up, watching it fall.

Midmorning, we went out for a hike through the BLM. With the layer of new snow, I found it surprisingly hard to recognize the draws and hillsides I had become so familiar with. There was such beauty in the mathematics of nature—the curving draws that bend and meet up with other draws like veins. We moved through them, running down the bottom of the draws, the red dirt angling up on either side. We crested a draw and jogged through the middle of a sagebrush flat and Charlie stopped for no reason other than to lean against my leg for a moment. The cool air brushed my cheeks; I leaned down and rubbed his side, the pressure of his body against my leg. He looked up at me, licked my cheek once, and then we were off again. On our way back to the house, Charlie found a fresh deer leg bone. He stopped, and began to gnaw on it. "Bring it," I said to him. "Bring it home," and Charlie picked up the bone and ran all the way back to the house, into the yard, and flopped down in the new snow to chew on it in ecstasy. Eli showed up shortly after, and I watched them out the window, sharing it side by side.

When Charlie came in and stretched out for an afternoon nap, I checked the progress of his castration. As I gently nudged aside the banded section to check for any sign of infection, it dropped to the carpet, a slight touch all that was needed to close the process. I dabbed Charlie's skin with peroxide, but Charlie didn't stir, didn't seem to notice at all.

That night, Charlie came inside in the early evening to eat and play. After he finished with his dinner, he walked slowly to where I sat typing and stood beside me with his ears folded on his head and licked his lips several times, looked up at me, and nuzzled my leg like he was saying *Thank you* for the food. It lasted only a moment, but I realized he had been doing this little ritual after eating every night for a week.

After finishing the paragraph I was working on, I got up to play with Charlie in the living room as we did every night, playing fetch and tug with his toys, and finishing with his favorite game of being chased around the coffee table. Charlie was so fast, and as I ran tight circles chasing him, he'd dodge to the left and leap over the couch, spin back, and then round the coffee table again as I kept the chase. After a few such laps, he rounded the coffee table with me inches behind him, faked to the left, but kept running straight. I kept running straight as well, because I never followed him over the sofa, and in this way, I accidentally stepped on his foot.

He stopped and looked at me, shocked. My mind raced with calculations of how far I was from the antler and what was the quickest route to get to it, when Charlie suddenly dropped his head and cowered onto his shoulder, then rolled completely over onto his back. I laughed inside as I knelt down to rub his favorite spot. This was the best proof of all that Charlie now saw me as the alpha.

· · ·

Charlie's fence arrived in boxes and bundles in the third week of March, and on Easter, a friend and I put it up. I tied Charlie on a shorter lead in the center of the yard so he was able to watch us without interfering with the work or feeling threatened by a stranger getting too close to him. I had noticed, in the past weeks, that Charlie was calm around strange people and things once he saw I was calm around them—I had even made a point of leaning against the UPS truck when it came down the driveway to show Charlie it was not a threat—and as long as he had his own space. Charlie watched us the whole time, alert but not panicked, as we drove in the corner posts, set up the charger box, and unrolled the netting, pulling it taut as we drove in the attached fence posts. We secured the ends to the house itself and the fence was up in half a day's time.

I avoided introducing Charlie to the fence that afternoon. I was exhausted and the wind was coming up, and I wanted to be fully rested and capable when we took that step. That night, after our evening walk, I left Charlie tied in his usual spot, where he was out of reach of the fence but would have the night to get used to it visually.

The next morning, I took Charlie out for our walk as usual. It was snowing again, just the very beginnings of it; the ground was half dusted like powdered-sugar snow. We stuck to the tight, low draws that zig-zagged out from one another. Charlie was on high speed, racing like a torpedo over the butt ends of the draws, making the fine red dirt fly and mingle with the falling snow, his ears back tight against his head, joy and freedom and fun splashed across his face. While Charlie napped inside, the sun came out, and by the time he woke, the snow was gone. I put Charlie on his leash, and together, we went out to meet the fence.

Charlie and I walked around in the new area, then traveled the perimeter, keeping a few feet in from the fence. Halfway around, Charlie, as I knew was inevitable, tiptoed up to the fence, looked and it, then reached out and sniffed it with his little wet nose. He yelped with the shock and immediately jumped backwards away from the fence. He stood stone still for a split second, then took off running in tight circles, his back end lowered, all the while looking around for "what did it," as if he had been stung by a bee. When he stopped his manic racing, he sat down and let me pet him, but he hunkered the whole time in an extreme-submissive posture that I had only ever seen him do when he was cornered by Mike's dogs. He then ran back to what he knew as his safe area in the yard in front of house and lay down in the shade. I tied him to the tree, gave him some water, and let him rest.

I went back outside a few hours later. Together, we walked the fence line. Charlie was happy and playful with me, but at the far edge of the enclosure, he sniffed at the fence again, and got zapped again. This was followed with the same yelp and wild run, but this time with real fear in his eyes—Charlie saw the fence in every direction and I could tell he felt trapped. He stopped in the very center of the fenced area behind the house and squatted with diarrhea, then ran to the safe area he understood. When I approached him, he bared his teeth but didn't growl; I didn't take it personally as I knew it was his defense from being scared. But I didn't push it. I tied him up, got my writing, and sat in the grass in his line of sight about three feet from fence, hoping to show him it was safe to be near the fence, just not touching it. Charlie stayed close to the house, obviously nervous. He didn't move all evening. I worked outside for an hour or so, and after taking care of some work in the house, I returned outside and sat near Charlie and talked to him. At dusk, he finally came over to me, warily sniffed my toe, then my leg, then my hand, saw that no shock was involved, and collapsed against my leg in need of love and comfort. I gave him a head, neck, and back massage to ease his tension from getting shocked. Charlie sat in front of me in serene delight while I massaged him; then, at the end, while

I lightly petted him from his head down the length of back, he moved his front paws to the left six inches to lean sideways a bit and expose his belly for me to rub. And when I did, he fell gently onto the ground, onto his back, with his front paws folded on his chest.

Charlie spent the night outside as usual, and again I tied him to the tree so he would not have a run-in with the fence during the night. He was happily frolicking in the yard the next morning when I let him inside and called out the kitchen door for Eli, who had not been meowing to come in. I found Eli sitting next to the house in obvious distress—he must have gotten zapped too, for he was far more affectionate than usual that morning. I gave them both extra meat and goat milk to counter the stress in their bodies, then sat down to work while Charlie played with his toys in the living room and Eli sat like a king on the sofa. Eventually, Charlie wore himself out and lay sprawled across his dog bed with a toy lamb in his mouth and slept.

When Charlie woke full of energy several hours later, we went outside together. Charlie slowly followed me around the fenced area, sniffing the ground in curiosity, though he stayed six feet away from the fence at all times. After an hour of slow and methodical exploration, he seemed to loosen up a bit, and as night fell, we ran in great circles, playing chase in the open area beside the house.

The next morning, I let Charlie in to say good morning to Eli and me, and then, as creamy pastels smothered across the sky and land, I let Charlie out into the yard without the leash. It was a huge step for me, but I forced myself not to be nervous. Every fifteen minutes, I got up from my computer and went out to check on him, and each time, Charlie was merrily prancing through the grass, pouncing on bugs or tossing his bones in the air. He came in for a nap, and after he and the cat slept for the morning, the three of us went outside. My breath caught at the simple luxury of opening the sliding glass door for all three of us to walk freely outside together. Charlie meandered around his new space, Eli lounged under a budding lilac, and I lay in the half-green grass, feeling content and at peace.

That night, I had a choice. I was still uncomfortable leaving Charlie outside all night untethered, but I didn't want to tie him up again after the gift of freedom we had waited so long for. I brought him in to spend the night inside, and went to bed, closed the bedroom door behind me, curious again for what the morning would hold.

I woke up, got dressed, and when I emerged from my bedroom, Charlie was waiting for me in the hallway, crouched on his belly, his ears folded on his head. We looked at each other. I was face-to-face with so many images, so many experiences I had had with him throughout the year we had spent together, from the first mornings when he drowsily woke beside me, to waking with his eager kisses as he squirmed between Mike and me in Mike's bed, to the snarls and fangs I had confronted in this very hallway. Charlie started whimpering, and as I walked toward him, he rolled over onto his back. I showered him with love and kisses and rubs, and he covered my face in delicate coyote licks.

Thirteen

April

Mornings have always been my favorite time of day, and now that Charlie spent the nights inside again, they were sweeter. I awoke to magical minor-key howls coming from the living room, Charlie's response to Eli meowing at the door. When Charlie heard my bedroom door open, he ran down the hall to greet me, tail wagging, to lick my face, his fur soft against my bare legs. We made our way back down the hallway, Charlie prancing in circles around my legs, to let Eli in. At Eli's entrance, Charlie's tail beat overtime and he dove toward the cat with worship in his eyes to sniff and nuzzle Eli's face, walking backwards as Eli tried to cross the room. Eli purred and wove between my ankles as we lavished him with attention.

They both followed me back down the hallway to the bathroom to watch me brush my teeth and wash my face; Eli crouched on the rim of the toilet seat and Charlie stood next to me with his pointy front paws on the edge of the sink. The three of us returned to the kitchen, where I gave Eli a bowl of goat milk and Charlie an egg. While I made coffee, Charlie and Eli tussled in the living room until Eli curled up on the sofa to sleep and Charlie scratched at the door, ready to explore the outdoors while I took care of the morning's work on the computer.

By the first week of April, spring had arrived. The lilacs were in bloom, the otherworldly call of the sandhill cranes carried over from the creek across the road, and the first butterflies danced in the sunlight. My work, though intense, was going smoothly. My days were dictated by the book manuscript, and by April 1 I had sent the full first draft to my editor and immediately dove headlong into the revisions. Photographs for The Daily Coyote provided a much-needed break from writing; though I still had the pressure of performing, of sending out a worthy photo each day, it was a time to let go of words and use a different part of myself; to play outside with Charlie, camera in hand, or creep up beside him on my belly as he slept to capture his peaceful smile.

In March, I had been contacted by a woman on the East Coast who had found my blog. She was a licensed wildlife rehabber, and every spring she nurtured coyote pups, raccoons, and a variety of other animals until they were strong and capable enough, thanks to her methodical care, to be released back into the wild. We struck up a correspondence and through the passing comments she made about her work, I learned what a delicate and systematic process it took to rehab animals for release. She offered to send me the vaccinations I needed for Charlie, including rabies. Her offer was a blessing, a gift for my own peace of mind, which I accepted with unexpressible gratitude.

When the vaccines arrived in the mail at the beginning of April, I opened the box, looked at all the vials and syringes, put them back in the box, and put the box in the fridge. I didn't have the courage to give Charlie the shots, not because I was nervous about how Charlie would react, but because I was so afraid of screwing up. Several days later, I took a noontime break from writing and saw Charlie sprawled on his bed, deep in a nap in a wash of sunlight. *There will never be a more opportune moment,* I said to myself, and went to the kitchen to prepare the rabies vaccine. I opened a syringe, pierced the long needle into a tiny glass vial of diluent and drew out the liquid. I plunged it into a matching vial that held the killed-virus vaccine and activated it. I knelt beside Charlie and rubbed his neck and back, then grasped the scruff at his neck. He didn't rustle. When I slid the needle under his skin, Charlie started but didn't get up, and relaxed under my hands as I depressed the plunger, then immediately fell back asleep.

The deer antler had become part of the living room decor on the floor at the end of the sofa. I no longer carried around any fear, but nor did I forget what Charlie was capable of. I was aware of the fact that there might be things I would never understand about him, or times when he felt poorly or was taken by surprise, or reacted in fear to something unpredictable. I placed deer antlers and small elk antlers around the house and yard; not only were they naturally beautiful, they were strategically placed defenses should I ever need them.

The second week of April, I noticed that baby bunnies had been born inside an old irrigation pipe that lay in the pasture just feet outside the electric netting, and when they emerged to nibble grass, Charlie paced the fence, desire in his every movement, yet he remained contained. Though Charlie never tested the fence, after a few days of watching Charlie obsessively watch the bunnies, I moved their pipe to the far end of the pasture, just for everyone's peace of mind.

During the day, I usually left the sliding door open so Charlie could come and go as he wished, and often he would trot in for no reason other than to stand beside me as I typed with one hand and rubbed his belly with the other, a brief visit and moment to connect, then return to his outdoor domain. He still chose to take his midday naps inside, and sometimes I joined him on the floor, to lazily burrow into his fur after a particularly difficult section of the book.

I still checked on him at intervals when he was outside; sometimes I'd find him racing around at top speed, tossing his toys in the air, a grin spread across his face; other times I'd spot him in the tall grass at the far reaches of the back pasture, catching grasshoppers, intent on his task and oblivious to me. Sometimes he simply stretched out in the very center of his new area, content to chew on a bone in the late afternoon sun. I was so happy to see him so happy, moving and doing as he pleased.

I took some revisions outside to work on by hand, and at one point I glanced up and saw Charlie stalking a meadowlark that sat on a fence post at the far edge of his fenced area. Charlie's body was lowered; he slowly, deliberately advanced through the grass, his eyes never leaving the bird. "Charlie," I called. He stopped, turned his head to look at me, and left his stalk to trot over to where I sat. His obedience was consistent. If he felt mischievous and grabbed the phone or some other forbidden object, the words *"Drop it"* from me, even from across the room, caused him to set it on the floor and let me take it. He easily gave up his toys when we played our hybrid version of fetch-and-chase; he was perfectly obedient with *"come"* and *"sit,"* and *"down"* had become obsolete, for he never jumped up on me anymore. I felt Charlie's easy and obliging behavior was indicative of his peace—both with me and the attitude I had achieved, and his new space and the freedom that came with it.

In mid-April, I started helping Mike feed again. Most of his calves had been born, and they hopped through the pasture on long, knobby legs beside their mothers, their glossy coats glinting in the afternoon sun. As the mother cows ate, calves tentatively sampled the hay with their lavender tongues before greedily returning to the udder. One afternoon after feeding the cows, Mike and I drove by the adjacent pasture so Mike could show me the new bulls he'd gotten. Two of the bulls were fighting, their heads slamming together, a cloud of dust kicked up around them.

"All bulls do is fight and eat and get carnal with the cows," I said. "Isn't that like every man's ideal life?"

"Ha!" Mike laughed. " 'Cept every six years, they're sold off and turned into hamburger and a new, younger bull comes in to take their place." He paused. "Isn't that like every woman's ideal life?"

We looked at each other across the pickup and laughed at the jokes and because it was so nice to be together again.

"So tell me what's going on with Charlie," Mike said, and I launched into tales of Charlie's latest antics; how he had learned to turn on the faucet of the bathroom sink; how, if I left a shirt in the living room, he would grab it and hold one corner of it in his mouth and spin in circles on his back feet like a cutting horse, and the shirt, arms and everything, would fly out parallel to the ground as he went round and round and round.

"These stories make me happy," he said, "that you two are back to where you were when he was just a bitty pup, shorter than a step."

I smiled at him.

"I was jealous and mad when you left," he said, "but Charlie wasn't even himself when you weren't with him, when he was up at my house. I'm glad that you were strong enough to go, and to make it happen."

"He still remembers you," I said. "When we're outside together, sometimes he'll just stop in the middle of whatever he's doing and look out toward the road, and every time, it's your truck he hears, and I can see you driving into town."

"That makes me feel good," Mike said, and paused with the thought. "So, you wanna see puppies?"

Pita, Mike's hound and Charlie's old friend, had accidentally been bred and a few weeks earlier she had crept into the chicken house and had a litter of nine puppies. There were two males and seven females, and they all looked different from one another. One matched Pita's brindle striping, two were classic border collie black-and-white, three had wavy black hair and looked like little bears, one was a sleek black shorthair, one was all white except for black bandit markings on her face, and the last was a mixture of black, white, and tan. The puppies had opened their eyes and were just beginning to explore, and they clambered over our feet and nuzzled into my neck as I held them, one by one. Their milk breath took me back to Charlie's first days with me in a wave of nostalgia.

"I guess I've got about a month and a half," I said to Mike with a smile, "to decide if I want to bring home a sister for Charlie."

"Yep," he said. "And you have pick of the litter."

"I've got to get back to work," I sighed, as I set the puppy I cradled among her squirming litter mates. "But I'll see you tomorrow?"

"I hope so," he said.

In late April, I went outside to watch the full moon rise over the red hills. Charlie moved gracefully through the grassy pasture; more so, it seemed, than he always had. I watched him, silent, swift, aware, as he spotted me across the yard and trotted over, his tail gracefully floating behind him like a plume. In his movements, in his eyes, he had a depth that kept pulling me further into him, further into myself. He had been with me for exactly a year. Time felt so nebulous, more like a figure eight than a linear streak. I couldn't believe how much had happened in such a short while, and yet I could barely remember how life felt before he was a part of mine. I sat in a lush patch of new grass, stroking Charlie as he lay beside me, watching the late light soften into pastels of dusk across the sky, and I thought, *Nothing is more perfect than April, and new beginnings.*

Acknowledgments

My thanks, and so much more, to Mike, for everything you have brought into my life. My gratitude and trust to Marysue Rucci, I could never have dreamed of a more wonderful editor. An eternal ovation to Stacey Glick, my rockstar of an agent. Love to Martha, Malia, and Karin for your sweetness and support.

Lasting gratitude to *Blockbuster Plots* by Martha Alderson, invaluable in getting my thoughts into book form; to George G., for helping make a hard decision so very simple; to Catherine F., for the quirky tips, which were more helpful than you will ever know; and to Phyllis W., for your experience and truest perceptions and the manner in which you share them.

And a grand hug to the internet, and a bow to all the individuals who visit The Daily Coyote. The notes you have sent me have changed my life; you have held me in awe.

Bibliography

Andrews, Ted. *Animal Speak*. Woodbury, Minn.: Llewellyn Publications, 1993.

Millan, Cesar. *Be The Pack Leader*. New York: Random House, 2007.

Rushdie, Salman. *The Ground Beneath Her Feet*. New York: Henry Holt & Company, 1999.

Stockton, Shreve. *Eating Gluten Free*. New York: Perseus Books Group, 2005.

The Daily Coyote:
A Story of Love, Survival, and Trust
in the Wilds of Wyoming

Discussion Questions

1. What does Shreve mean when she says "animals kept me accountable in a way that was all too easy to skirt when living alone or interacting only with people"? Provide specific examples of the ways that animals keep her accountable. Why do you believe animals rather than people have that power over Shreve?

2. Shreve's beliefs about death differ markedly from Mike's and impact how they each approach life and its challenges. Explain the differences you perceive. Is one of their approaches comparable to your own? Why?

3. Why do you believe that people subscribed to The Daily Coyote? What did Shreve learn about these subscribers when Charlie became ill? How do their feelings about Charlie contrast with Shreve's own recognition of his value to her? Would you subscribe to The Daily Coyote? Why or why not?

4. Describe Charlie's development under Shreve's care. How do his developmental milestones both parallel and challenge Shreve's personal struggles with freedom and safety? How does Shreve's understanding and appreciation of the costs of freedom evolve over the course of the book?

5. Identify the contradictions inherent in Mike's life as a coyote hunter and a hunting guide. Why is he increasingly disillusioned by the hunters he takes on hunting trips? What do you think Shreve's thoughts about the dichotomy of urban versus rural living reveals about Mike's struggles? Do you agree with Shreve's conclusions about urban and rural living? Why or why not?

6. Shreve initially believes she has found a breakthrough in countering Charlie's increasing aggression toward her. What does she think underlies Charlie's progression from affection to anger? What lessons does she believe she needs to learn in order to make Charlie's life and her own life better? Is she successful? Why or why not?

7. How do you feel about Shreve adopting and raising a wild animal? What might you have done differently?

8. "Risking discipleship" is one of the messages that Shreve notices on the church's readerboard in her drive from town. What do you think this quote means? How does it relate to Shreve's own struggle to deal with her sudden notoriety? What do you believe are the risks and benefits of her online exposure?

9. Shreve finally turns a corner with Charlie's aggression when she becomes an "energetic alpha" for Charlie. Describe what she means by this term and how it impacts her overall approach to living her life. Do you agree with her rationale for why she was able to affect change in Charlie? Why or why not?

10. According to Shreve, there are "gifts of the dead" that can help humans become stronger. What do you believe are the gifts left by Tracy for Mike? Have you received your own 'gifts of the dead'? If yes, what are they? If no, why not?

11. Consider the relationship between Eli and Charlie. How does it evolve as the story progresses? How does Shreve's relationship with each of them differ? What does the evolution of their relationships reveal about nature and our potential place in it?

Author Q&A

You say that you have never felt roots, have never felt connected to family, religion, or any societal group. Has your sense of being rootless changed since you settled in Wyoming? What do you think is at the heart of your sense of not belonging?

I don't think there was any event or series of events that caused me to always feel like a "floater." I think it's just one of those traits I came here with from birth. It's allowed me to have the past that I've had, and it helped train my eye as a photographer and writer: since I didn't have allegiances to any particular group or "pack," I wasn't as governed by subconscious preconceptions or "loyalties" and could immerse myself in such a great range of experiences.

A part of this has changed, mellowed a bit, in the past few years. Charlie has much to do with that, grounding me; and what I've learned from living so close to the land and to nature has given me so much clarity. I certainly run outside of the normal parameters of society, still, but I am more centered in myself than I ever was before.

Why do you believe people responded to your daily pictures of Charlie? What do you believe he or your relationship with him represented for your email followers? What surprised you about the group?
I was amazed how quickly and solidly people—strangers—became emotionally invested in Charlie. I think because of my background in photography and my relationship with Charlie, his energy and personality has been able to shine through, so clearly and lively, in my photos of him. And people can connect to that—to that life and energy. He definitely provides different things for different people, but if I had to put it into one word, I would choose the word *wonder*. Charlie brings wonder. And wonder carries with it a soft hint of trust in possibility, and hope.

One of the great features of your book are the daily meditations on the Methodist Church readerboard that you encounter on your way home. What did these sayings mean to you? How did they serve to connect you to a larger story in the great expanse of Wyoming?
I love the readerboard messages because they were (are) so wildly creative, and they pushed my mind to see all the possible angles of what was being said in just a few words. Seeing all angles, all sides of a thing, has been a rich and important part of my experience here in this tiny town in Wyoming. I came, essentially, as a foreigner. I have been able to learn and grow so much by stretching my perceptions and not fixating on what I was used to or what I expected.

And I must share this aside here: a few weeks after my book was published, I drove by the church to find the readerboard proclaiming "Shreve—We Love Your Book." I was so incredibly honored!

As you struggled to pinpoint Charlie's increased aggression toward you, you tended to look mostly inside of yourself. Why?
I suppose I looked inside myself because if the cause was inside me, I would

be able to change it. If it had an external cause, there would be less of a chance that I would be able to fix it. And I have always had a deep conviction that the events we are presented with in our life are tailored to us—that they come to us for a reason, for growth or betterment, even if it's too devastating to see in the moment. And so I believed that Charlie's aggression, which was incredibly difficult and devastating for me, was something that was showing up in order to show me something about myself that I had been ignoring.

How has your relationship with Mike evolved?
Mike is so inspiring to me. He continues to push himself and his own boundaries and comfort zones, continues to actively strive to become stronger and more conscious, and continues to define what that means for him. In working on ourselves side by side, we work together, and our relationship becomes even more intimate and dynamic.

When you conquered your battle with Charlie's aggression, you termed the change you embodied as *energetic alpha*. Tell us more about the state this term designates and its characteristics. How might we apply this phenomenon beyond the human-animal relationship?
By energetic alpha I mean a solid, unwavering conviction in oneself. One that cannot be broken by intimidation from outside sources. It was essential for me to make this leap in myself so that I could project this conviction with every move and posture while working through Charlie's aggressive behavior. Humans can be fooled by words, but animals aren't. I had to have it in my very being.

Energetic alpha is a combination of confidence and grace, and this translates seamlessly to every area of life—personal and business relationships, even our attitudes regarding work and personal trials—and the manner in which we move through life.

How do you answer critics who believe that you do not fully appreciate that Charlie is a wild animal who will eventually act true to form and hurt someone, possibly you?
I never forget that Charlie is a wild animal. In fact, I have never referred to him as my pet. Keeping Charlie safe from others as well as keeping others safe from Charlie is a responsibility I take incredibly seriously. There are several posts on my website (www.dailycoyote.net) in which I discuss this in depth.